Patterns of Free
Trade Areas in Asia

Policy Studies

an East-West Center series

Series Editors: Edward Aspinall and Dieter Ernst

Description

Policy Studies presents scholarly analysis of key contemporary domestic and international political, economic, and strategic issues affecting Asia in a policy relevant manner. Written for the policy community, academics, journalists, and the informed public, the peer-reviewed publications in this series provide new policy insights and perspectives based on extensive fieldwork and rigorous scholarship.

The East-West Center is pleased to announce that the Policy Studies series has been accepted for indexing in the Web of Science Book Citation Index. The Web of Science is the largest and most comprehensive citation index available. The quality and depth of content Web of Science offers to researchers, authors, publishers, and institutions sets it apart from other research databases. The inclusion of Policy Studies in the Book Citation Index demonstrates our dedication to providing the most relevant and influential content to our community.

Notes to Contributors

Submissions may take the form of a proposal or complete manuscript. For more information on the Policy Studies series, please contact the Series Editors.

Editors, *Policy Studies*
East-West Center
1601 East-West Road
Honolulu, Hawai'i 96848-1601
Tel: 808.944.7197
Publications@EastWestCenter.org
EastWestCenter.org/PolicyStudies

Policy Studies 65

Patterns of Free Trade Areas in Asia

Masahiro Kawai and Ganeshan Wignaraja

Patterns of Free Trade Areas in Asia
Masahiro Kawai and Ganeshan Wignaraja

ISSN 1547-1349 (print) and 1547-1330 (electronic)
ISBN 978-0-86638-237-3 (print) and 978-0-86638-238-0 (electronic)

The views expressed are those of the author(s) and not necessarily those of the Center.

Hard copies of all titles, and free electronic copies of most titles, are available from:

Publication Sales Office
East-West Center
1601 East-West Road
Honolulu, Hawai'i 96848-1601
Tel: 808.944.7145
Fax: 808.944.7376
EWCBooks@EastWestCenter.org
EastWestCenter.org/PolicyStudies

In Asia, hard copies of all titles, and electronic copies of select Southeast Asia titles, co-published in Singapore, are available from:

Institute of Southeast Asian Studies
30 Heng Mui Keng Terrace
Pasir Panjang Road, Singapore 119614
publish@iseas.edu.sg
bookshop.iseas.edu.sg

Contents

List of Acronyms

ADB	Asian Development Bank
ADBI	Asian Development Bank Institute
AEC	ASEAN Economic Community
AFTA	ASEAN Free Trade Agreement
AMRO	ASEAN+3 Macroeconomic Research Office
APEC	Asia-Pacific Economic Cooperation
APTA	Asia-Pacific Trade Agreement
ARIC	Asia Regional Integration Center
ASEAN	Association of Southeast Asian Nations
CECA	Comprehensive Economic Cooperation Agreement
CEPA(s)	comprehensive economic partnership agreement(s)
CEPEA	Comprehensive Economic Partnership for East Asia
CGE	computable general equilibrium
EAFTA	East Asia Free Trade Area

ECOTECH	Economic and Technical Cooperation
EFTA	European Free Trade Area
EPA(s)	economic partnership agreement(s)
EU	European Union
FDI	foreign direct investment
FTA(s)	free trade agreement(s)
FTAA	Free Trade Area of the Americas
FTAAE	Free Trade Area of Asia and Europe
FTAAP	Free Trade Area of the Asia-Pacific
GATS	General Agreement on Trade in Services
GATS-plus FTAs	FTAs liberalizing services-trade policies beyond GATS commitments in relation to subsectors or regulations
GATT	General Agreement on Tariffs and Trade
GDP	gross domestic product
MFN(s)	most favored nation(s)
MNC(s)	multinational corporation(s)
MRA(s)	mutual recognition agreement(s)
NAFTA	North American Free Trade Agreement
P4	Pacific Four
PECC	Pacific Economic Cooperation Council
PPP	purchasing power parity
PTA(s)	preferential trade agreement(s)
RCEP	Regional Comprehensive Economic Partnership
ROO	rules of origin

SME(s)   small- and medium-sized enterprise(s)

TPP   Trans-Pacific Strategic Economic Partnership (also, Trans-Pacific Partnership)

US   United States (of America)

WTO   World Trade Organization

WTO-plus FTAs   FTAs including obligations exceeding the existing requirements of WTO agreements

Executive Summary

Asian economies face important policy challenges regarding the use of free trade agreements (FTAs): primarily their scope and their impact on economic growth and regionalization trends. These topics are the front line of contemporary negotiations and are currently of great interest to policymakers. This study reviews existing literature, provides new data from enterprise-level interviews on the business impacts of FTAs, and uses analytical tools to examine the contents of existing FTAs and economic (specifically, computable general equilibrium) modeling to highlight the economic impacts of existing FTAs.

Asia's rise as the "global factory" over several decades was underpinned by outward-oriented development strategies and multilateralism. FTAs, as trade-policy instruments in the region, were largely absent until the 1990s. Today Asia is a world leader, with 71 FTAs and more under development.

The region's largest economies (the Peoples' Republic of China [China], India, and Japan) and the Association of Southeast Asian Nations' (ASEANs') economies (e.g. Singapore and Thailand) have become key players in FTA activity. Smaller neighboring economies are now also actively involved in such efforts. Reflecting the growth of FTAs, the importance of FTAs to trade at the economy level has also increased.

The increase in FTAs is attributed to factors including the need to remove impediments to broadening the market-led integration of production networks, the intensification of FTA activity in Europe and the Americas, and the stalled World Trade Organization (WTO) Doha Round trade talks.

Concerns over such agreements have increased as FTAs have spread across Asia. Several key challenges associated with Asian FTAs are examined here, from a pragmatic perspective, with a view to providing better informed policy decisions.

While well-designed FTAs provide demonstrable benefits, previous studies document that the historic use of FTAs by Asian economies has been relatively low. New data, however, show that FTA preference use had risen significantly by 2011 to reach 61 percent of total exports in Thailand and 31 percent of total exports in Vietnam. Asian Development Bank/Asian Development Bank Institute (ADB/ADBI) surveys of China, Japan, Malaysia, Philippines, Singapore, South Korea, and Thailand also indicate higher-than-expected FTA use at enterprise-level with 32 percent of enterprises using FTAs and more planning to do so. The surveys also reveal that FTA use entails fixed costs and that large enterprises are able to muster the requisite financial and human resources better than small- and medium-sized enterprises (SMEs).

A lack of information on FTAs is identified as the most significant reason for non-use of FTAs. Low margins of preference, administrative costs and delays associated with rules of origin (ROO) and other export documentation, and non-tariff measures in partner economies were the other reasons cited for non-use of FTAs.

Existing literature suggests that multiple rules of origin in overlapping FTAs raise transaction costs for SMEs. ADB/ADBI surveys indicate that multiple ROO are a future risk to Asian enterprises rather than a present issue. These surveys also reveal that larger enterprises in Asia have more negative perceptions of multiple ROO than SMEs. Large established enterprises export to multiple markets and adapt their business strategies in response to FTAs. They are, therefore, more likely to express concerns regarding multiple ROOs. In contrast, SMEs tend to export to single markets and hence have little basis for complaint.

The literature shows that the coverage of agricultural trade differs markedly among current Asian FTAs. Agricultural products may have been substantially excluded from such agreements based on pressure from powerful farm lobbies or social concerns regarding poverty in rural areas.

Review of tariff-line coverage of agricultural products in current Asian FTAs shows that, over time, these agreements are becoming more comprehensive in their coverage of agricultural products. Of the 69 FTAs for which data were available in 2012, 46 percent had comprehensive coverage, another 28 percent had some coverage, and 26 percent had little or no coverage of agricultural products.

FTAs may also contribute to reducing the significant regulatory restrictions on services trade currently present in the region. Review of criteria covering key sectors of the General Agreement on Trade in Services (GATS) similarly indicates a trend in Asian FTAs towards progressively liberalizing the services-trade sectors of participants and providing, again over time, for increased regulatory cooperation on services trade. Of the 69 FTAs reviewed, 41 percent had comprehensive coverage, another 25 percent had some coverage, and 23 percent had little or no coverage of services trade.

Studies demonstrate that Asian FTAs vary considerably in their scope (e.g., the inclusion of issues going beyond the WTO framework). Review of criteria covering the four "Singapore issues" (competition, intellectual property, investment, and public procurement) shows that, of the 69 FTAs reviewed, 23 percent had comprehensive "WTO-plus" coverage, another 54 percent had partial WTO-plus coverage, and 23 percent were goods-and-services agreements only.

This study suggests several recommendations for the future. These include strengthening the systems providing support for enterprises, especially SMEs, using or wishing to use FTAs; rationalizing ROO and improving their administration; ensuring better coverage of agricultural trade; facilitating services-trade liberalization; forging comprehensive WTO-plus FTAs; and encouraging a region-wide FTA. Concluding the WTO Doha Round trade talks and reducing protectionism would also be invaluable in boosting FTA use.

A region-wide FTA would provide such economic benefits as increased market access for goods, services, skills, and technology; greater market size permitting increased specialization and greater realization of economies of scale; easier foreign direct investment and technology transfer by multinational corporations; simpler trade rules; and insurance against protectionist sentiments.

Rather than a single agreement, a region-wide FTA could arise from a series of linked agreements covering varied issues and participants. Two competing processes could become the future basis for a region-wide FTA: 1) a Regional Comprehensive Economic Partnership (RCEP) among the ASEAN +6 FTA (the 10 ASEAN economies plus Australia, China, India, Japan, New Zealand, and South Korea); and 2) the Trans-Pacific Strategic Economic Partnership (Trans-Pacific Partnership, or TPP) agreement among the eleven economies (Australia, Brunei Darussalam, Canada, Chile, Malaysia, Mexico, New Zealand, Peru, Singapore, United States, and Vietnam) currently in negotiations, plus Japan and other economies that have expressed interest in joining the negotiations.

To realize the RCEP, a trilateral FTA among China, Japan, and South Korea should first be concluded and then be connected with the existing ASEAN+1 FTAs. TPP aims to achieve high-quality agreements and includes Brunei Darussalam, Malaysia, Singapore, and Vietnam (and Japan, if pre-negotiation, bilateral consultations are successful) as Asian members. It has the potential to develop into a larger APEC-wide FTA—however that would require successfully first addressing the difficult task of forging a US-China FTA.

The biggest challenge lies in the political will of the various economies to face and overcome geopolitical considerations. The changing center of global economic gravity—given the rapid economic rise of China and India—suggests that a RCEP may be the preferred answer. Security considerations might, alternatively, drive some Asian economies to prefer a TPP as that answer would strengthen existing ties with the United States.

However these two processes are not mutually exclusive and might prove to be complementary. Whichever path or paths may be taken, it will be important to accelerate the liberalization of goods and services investment and trade, reduce behind-the-border barriers, and pursue domestic reforms. A harmonious Asia and Pacific trade area would likely require a convergence of the two processes being considered. This would be a win-win solution for the Asia Pacific community.

Patterns of Free Trade Areas in Asia

Introduction

The spread of new free trade agreements (FTAs) within Asia is affecting the region's trade policies and current status as the "global factory." This study addresses the policy issues that Asian economies face with regard to the use of Asian FTAs, the scope of these FTAs, and the impact of the FTAs on economic growth and Asian regionalization trends.

These topics are the core issues of current negotiations and should be of great interest to contemporary policymakers. This study reviews existing literature on these topics, provides new data from affected enterprises on the business impacts of these FTAs, analyzes the contents of current FTAs, and uses economic (specifically, computable general equilibrium) modeling to highlight their impacts.

The study focuses on three interrelated developments:

First, Asia's advanced production networks, underlying its emergence over the past several decades as the global factory, have broadened regionally (Kimura 2006, ADB 2008, Hiratsuka 2011). While production networks were temporarily disrupted in 2011 following Japan's triple disaster and Thailand's flooding, overall today's industrial production processes are devolving into smaller sub-processes with each sub-process locating in the most cost-effective economy, thereby improving efficiency.

Intraregional trade in Asia, particularly in the production of industrial parts and components, has significantly increased. While Asia has largely maintained low tariffs on industrial goods, other regulatory barriers (on competition, standards, investment, and services) still impede the further growth of production networks. Additional liberalization of regional regulatory barriers, through new FTAs, may facilitate the continued growth of production networks.

Second, Asia—a relative latecomer to the use of FTAs as trade-policy instruments—is now at the forefront of global FTA activity (Fiorentino, Crawford, and Toqueboeuf 2009; WTO 2011).

While the Association of Southeast Asian Nations' (ASEANs') 10 (currently Brunei Darussalam, Cambodia, Indonesia, Lao People's Democratic Republic [Lao PDR], Malaysia, Myanmar, Philippines, Singapore, Thailand, and Vietnam) more-developed economies emerged as the initial hub for Asian FTAs, other major Asian economies are now also actively developing FTAs (Urata 2004, Kawai 2005, Chia 2010, Kawai and Wignaraja 2008 and 2011a, Zhang and Shen 2011). In May 2012 negotiations began on a People's Republic of China (China)–South Korea FTA and official discussions started on a China-Japan-South Korea FTA.

With additional economies now expressing interest in such negotiations, interest in the Trans-Pacific Strategic Economic Partnership (also, Trans-Pacific Partnership, or TPP) appears to be growing as an alternative hub for Asian FTA integration (Petri, Plummer, and Zhai 2011; Gordon 2012; Lim, Elms, and Low 2012). The United States has executed strategic bilateral FTAs with Singapore and South Korea while the European Union (EU) has a completed FTA with South Korea. As the World Trade Organization (WTO) Doha Round trade talks have stalled (as of the time of this writing), many more FTAs are currently under negotiation and there is little sign of any diminishing Asian enthusiasm for FTAs.

Third, there is an emerging body of literature on policy issues concerning Asian FTAs.[1] Issues and concerns highlighted in recent literature include the limited utilization of FTA preferences, a "noodle bowl" problem of crisscrossing agreements that potentially may distort trade toward bilateral channels, excessive exclusions and specified special treatments, limited liberalization of agriculture and service trades, and the possibility that the multilateral trading system may be progressively eroded (Baldwin 2006, Tumbarello 2007, World Bank 2007, Bhagwati 2008, Drysdale and Armstrong 2010, Hoekman and Mattoo 2011).

As FTAs are relatively new to Asian economies, previously limited empirical evidence (particularly with respect to patterns of Asian FTAs and their business impacts) has made it difficult to establish the validity or lack thereof of these concerns. With the increased availability of recent data it is now possible to develop an evidence-based assessment of Asian FTAs.

Recent data make it now possible to develop an assessment of Asian FTAs

FTA-led regionalism in Asia appears likely to continue for three reasons.

First, the large economies of Northeast Asia—China, Japan, and South Korea—are at the forefront of the use of FTAs to pursue their respective regional and global trade strategies. ASEAN members are increasingly entering into FTAs as a means to expand their investment and trade opportunities and increase their participation in Asia's advanced production networks.

Second, the currently stalled World Trade Organization (WTO) Doha Round trade talks means that FTAs are particularly attractive as immediately available vehicles to support the broadening of production networks through investment and trade liberalization.

Finally, even if the Doha Round trade talks were to be concluded in the near future, FTA activity would likely continue as many of the "new age" FTAs go well beyond what is on the Doha Round negotiating table. These "new age" FTAs also address competition, intellectual property, investment, and public procurement (often referred to as "the Singapore issues"). Accordingly, Asian enterprises now need to learn to export more effectively under a regional trade regime based upon FTAs. The focus for Asian policymakers must be how best to minimize the costs of FTAs (e.g., administrative and transactional costs) while maximizing the benefits (e.g., better market access, new business opportunities, and preferential tariffs).

This study pragmatically examines patterns and challenges in Asian FTAs with a view to offering policy guidance.

"Mapping Asian Free Trade Agreements" summarizes Asia's emergence as the global factory through outward-oriented development strategies and highlights the region's recent emphasis on FTAs. It charts major trends in Asian FTAs since 2000, including activity intensity, cross-regional orientation, growth, and trade coverage.

"Challenges Posed by Asian Free Trade Agreements" analyzes six key challenges posed by Asian FTAs: 1) increasing the use of FTA preferences, 2) tackling the Asian noodle bowl problem, 3) promoting the comprehensive coverage of agricultural trade, 4) facilitating services-trade liberalization, 5) inclusion of new issues (e.g., competition) that go beyond the WTO framework, and 6) forming a region-wide FTA. New evidence from the analysis of FTAs, enterprise-level surveys, and computable general equilibrium (CGE) models are used to analyze these challenges.

In response to increasing interest in forming a region-wide agreement, "Political-Economy Considerations of Asian Free Trade Agreements" explores political economy issues as they relate to FTA consolidation in Asia and the potential connection of such consolidated Asian FTAs with both Europe and the North Americas.

The study's conclusion advocates strengthening the support system for regional production networks, forging comprehensive "WTO-plus" FTAs, and encouraging an Asia-wide FTA in the form of RCEP and TPP. An expectation for the success of a "bottom-up" approach to the WTO Doha Round trade talks emerges from the analysis.[2]

Mapping Asian Free Trade Agreements

Emergence of the Global Factory

Asia's rise over a fifty-year period from a poor and underdeveloped agricultural backwater to becoming the global factory is now widely recognized as an impressive economic achievement (World Bank 1993, Stiglitz 1996 and 2001, ADB 2008 and 2010).

In the 1960s, however, developing Asian economies lacked natural resources and had high levels of poverty. There seemed little prospect of rapid economic advancement. In *Asian Drama*, Myrdal (1968) famously presented a pessimistic view of Asia's development prospects. Myrdal described a region mired in a vicious cycle of poverty and hindered (particularly in agriculture) by unfavorable initial conditions, institutions, and politics. He questioned the ability of the market to produce equitable growth and development. History has clearly disproven such pessimistic predictions from Myrdal and others.

Several factors have been crucial in Asia's successful industrialization and structural transformation. Developing Asian economies had ample supplies of low-cost highly productive labor. These developing economies were also geographically close to an already developed and expanding high-income country, Japan. Efficient Japanese multinational corporations (MNCs) were actively seeking to relocate production operations to less costly locations in Asia.

Asian multilateralism—supported through the WTO framework and its predecessor, the General Agreement on Tariffs and Trade (GATT)—and open regionalism—supported by unilateral liberalization by individual economies with intellectual support from the Asia-Pacific Economic Cooperation (APEC) trade group—underpinned much of Asia's approach to international trade policy for several decades.

This approach resulted in historically low average Asian most favored nation (MFN) tariffs of 10.8 percent by 2000—and these tariffs fell further to 7.4 percent by 2010 (Appendix Table 1).[3] At individual-economy levels international trade policy was anchored by the creation of strong infrastructure, outward-oriented development strategies, high domestic savings rates, and major investments in human capital (World Bank 1993). A booming world economy hungry for

Asian multilateralism has underpinned Asia's approach to international trade policy for decades

low-cost labor-intensive imports, falling tariffs in developed markets, inflows of trade-related foreign direct investment (FDI), and generous inflows of foreign aid also favored outward-oriented growth in Asia.

Decades of market-driven expansion of trade and FDI, during which Asia increasingly became a global production center with deep and diverse technological capabilities, followed. Baldwin (2006) aptly refers to "factory Asia" while others chose to identify Asia as the global factory.

Using strategies of innovation and learning, Asian enterprises acquired the requisite technological capabilities to either compete with or become suppliers to various MNCs (Hobday 1995, Mathews and

Cho 2000, Ernst 2004, Wignaraja 2012a). Asian enterprises developed production-engineering skills efficiently using imported technologies and successfully fitting themselves into the advanced global production networks formed by other local suppliers and MNCs. As systematic innovation and learning took place at the enterprise level, a shift from labor-intensive exports (e.g., footwear, garments, and textiles) to more technology-intensive exports (e.g., automobiles, chemicals, electric appliances, electronics, and ships) occurred (Lall 2000). Some Asian enterprises generated significant innovative capabilities with investments in research and development, emerging as leading enterprises in production networks and supply chains.

Some have argued, perhaps controversially, that the creation of enterprise-level technological capabilities and industrial competitiveness was carefully and proactively nurtured by Asian economies including China, Singapore, South Korea, and Taiwan (Wade, 1990, Lall 1992, Lin 2012). The argument goes that these economies identified and facilitated the development of industries where they found a competitive advantage and used these industries as a basis for economic development.

Trade within Asia increased from 37% of total trade in 1980 to 54% in 2011

Furthermore, these scholars argued that trade liberalization was accompanied by financial policies to generate high savings rates, investments in education and physical infrastructure, efficient science and technology institutions, aggressive attraction of foreign direct investment and, in some cases, incentives for the development of particular industries.

Rising Asian economic prosperity followed the rapid industrialization. Asia's share of world gross domestic product (GDP) in purchasing power parity (PPP) more than doubled from 16 percent in 1980 to 33 percent by 2011 (Appendix Table 1). Five of the world's richest economies—in terms of PPP per-capita income—are now in Asia: Hong Kong (Special Administrative Region, China), Japan, Singapore, South Korea, and Taiwan.

Falling Asian regional trade barriers and logistics costs, technological progress, and rising costs in other production locations spurred the decentralization of production networks to the most cost-effective locations (Athukorala 2011, Hiratsuka 2011). Trade within Asia increased from 37 percent of total trade in 1980 to 54 percent by 2011. This increase was led by trade in industrial parts and components (see www.aric.adb.org/databases/integration indicators).

Nearing the close of the twentieth century the Asian story of export success and outward orientation was altered by a growth in FTAs which changed the nature of Asia's international trade policies.

Growth of FTAs

FTAs were largely absent in Asia until the 1990s. The Asia-Pacific Trade Agreement (APTA),[4] which took effect in 1976, was the region's first such agreement. It was followed by the Thailand–Lao PDR Preferential Trade Agreement (PTA) in 1991 and the ASEAN Free Trade Agreement (AFTA) in 1992.

With the emerging multilateralism, Asia began emphasizing FTAs as a trade-policy instrument in the 1990s and the region is today at the forefront of world FTA activity (Feridhanusetyawan 2005; Fiorentino, Crawford, and Toqueboeuf 2009). A comprehensive review by the WTO (2011) of the evolution of the international FTA landscape notes:

> ...the countries of Asia have only recently become active in signing preferential trade agreements (PTAs). Over the last 10 years, countries in East and West Asia, as well as Oceania have participated in almost half the PTAs concluded over that period (more than, for instance, European and CIS countries, which participated in one-third of agreements), while their participation in PTA activities in the 1990s barely reached 5 percent (only 6 out of 106 agreements).

The Asian Development Bank's (ADB's) Asia Regional Integration Center (ARIC) FTA Database (www.aric.adb.org) provides information on the number of concluded FTAs in Asia (as of September 2012). The significant expansion of Asian FTAs occurred during the 2000s. As Figure 1 shows, the number of concluded FTAs in Asia collectively increased from 3 to 22 between 2000 and 2005 and still further to 71 by 2012. Sixty-four of these FTAs are currently in effect.

This figure, according to the WTO (2011), compares with around three hundred FTAs world-wide. The proliferation of FTAs in Asia is

Figure 1. Growth of Concluded* FTAs in Asia,** 1976–2012
(Number of FTAs)

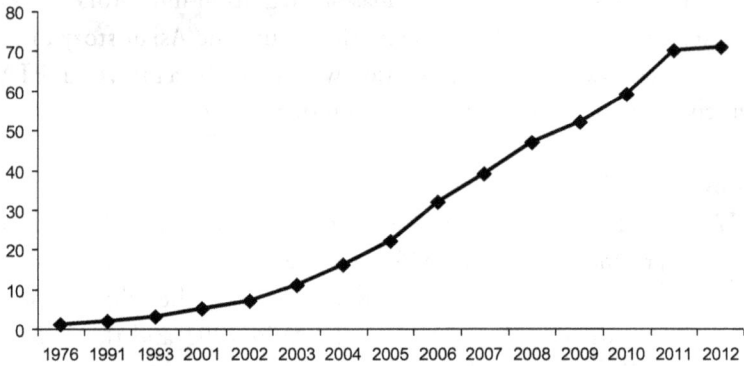

Source: ARIC FTA Database (www.aric.adb.org); data as of September 2012.
Notes: * Concluded FTAs include those currently in effect and those that have been
signed but are not yet in effect.
** Asia (as used here) includes the ten ASEAN economies and China, Hong Kong,
India, Japan, South Korea, and Taiwan.

likely to be sustained—an additional 84 are either proposed or under
negotiation.

Asian economies appear to be choosing bilateral agreements rather
than more complex multilateral agreements. This may well be because bilateral agreements are generally easier to negotiate. Bilateral
FTAs comprise 76 percent of Asia's concluded FTAs while multilateral FTAs comprise only the remaining 24 percent.

Four main factors underlie the recent spread of FTA initiatives in
Asia: 1) deepening market-driven economic integration in Asia, 2)
European and North American economic integration, 3) the 1997–
98 Asian financial crisis, and 4) the current lack of progress in the
WTO Doha Round trade talks.[5]

First among these is market-driven economic integration through
FDI, trade, and the formation of Asian production networks and
supply chains. Market-driven economic integration has begun to require further liberalization of FDI and trade and harmonization of
policies, rules, and standards governing FDI and trade—including
the protection of intellectual property rights and investments. Asia's
policymakers are increasingly of the view that FTAs, if given wide
scope, support expanding FDI and trade activities through further

elimination of cross-border impediments and other such harmonization efforts. Thus FTAs are regarded as elements of a supportive policy framework for deepening production networks and supply chains formed by global MNCs and emerging Asian enterprises.

Second, European and North American economic integration—including European Union (EU) expansion into central and eastern Europe, a monetary union in the Eurozone, the success of the North American Free Trade Agreement (NAFTA), and incipient moves toward a Free Trade Area of the Americas (FTAA)—motivated Asian economies to adopt FTAs.

Asian economies fear that the two giant trading blocs of Europe and North America might dominate rule-setting in the global trading system, thereby marginalizing Asia. Increasingly policymakers have realized the need for stepping up the pace of Asian integration to improve international competitiveness by exploiting economies of scale and strengthening their bargaining power through a collective voice on global trade issues. FTAs provide an alternative to the periodic difficulties, such as the current lack of progress in the WTO Doha Round trade talks and a perceived lack of progress in the voluntary APEC process, inherent in multilateral trade liberalization.

Third, the 1997–98 Asian financial crisis made it clear that Asian economies need to work together in the areas of investment and trade to sustain regional growth and stability by addressing common challenges. This need has not yet been fully met either by existing regional initiatives to strengthen the international economic system or by economy-level efforts to strengthen the fundamentals of individual economies. Both efforts will take additional time to bear fruit. The proliferation of FTA initiatives within the Asian region has encouraged a number of economies to participate rather than face exclusion.

Fourth, the current lack of progress in the WTO Doha Round trade talks has encouraged economies to consider FTAs as attractive and accessible alternatives. Initially hailed as a development round to promote trade-led growth in poor economies, the WTO Doha Round trade talks began over a decade ago in November 2001. The talks have largely focused on liberalization in two key areas: agricultural- and non-agricultural-products market access.

In essence, developed economies were being asked to accelerate the pace and scope of reductions in agricultural tariffs and subsidies while developing economies were being asked to reduce industrial tariffs and subsidies and liberalize services trade. Seven years of formal negotiations eventually stalled in mid-2008 over concerns in developing economies addressing safeguard measures to protect poor farmers from rising food and oil prices.

Discussions have, however, continued behind the scenes. It now appears likely that the Doha Round trade talks will not be particularly comprehensive even if they are ever concluded. As prospects for a substantive and timely agreement diminished over the years, pro-business Asian economies emphasized bilateral and multilateral FTAs for the continued liberalization of trade in goods and services as well as the adoption of the Singapore issues (i.e., competition, intellectual property, investment, and public procurement), which are currently beyond the scope of the WTO discussions.

Intensity of FTA Activity in Asia

Despite of the increase in FTAs in Asia since 2000, the region has fewer FTAs per economy relative to international levels. Asia has an average of nine FTAs per economy compared to a global average of 13 FTAs to which each WTO member is a party (Appendix Table 1, WTO 2011). Asian FTA activity over the last decade has given rise to a varying number of agreements per economy.

> *The region's three largest economies and the more-developed ASEAN economies have become particularly active in FTAs*

As Figure 2 shows, the region's three largest economies and the more-developed ASEAN economies have become particularly active in FTAs. Smaller Asian economies have less frequently participated in FTAs.

Asian economies with numerous concluded FTAs include Singapore (20), India (13), Japan (13), China (12), Malaysia (12), and Thailand (12). More FTAs are currently under negotiation. However, for comparison, the EU is the world's leader in concluded FTAs with 31 and the United States has 20 (Appendix Table 1).

It is noteworthy that ASEAN—with one of the oldest trade agreements in Asia—is emerging as the major hub linking ASEAN

Figure 2. Increase in Concluded FTAs in Asia, 2000 and 2012
(Number of FTAs by Economy)

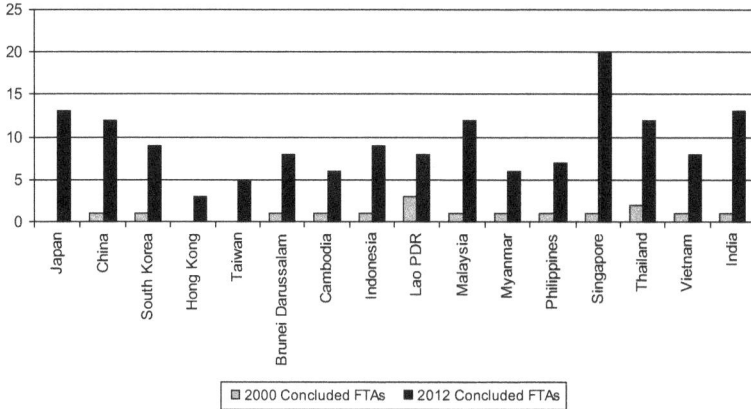

Source: ADB, ARIC FTA Database (www.aric.adb.org), data as of September 2012.
Note: Asia (as used here) includes the 16 economies identified in the figure. "FTAs in Asia" includes those FTAs involving at least one of these Asian economies.

members with the region's larger economies. Having enacted FTAs with China, Japan, and South Korea, ASEAN recently implemented regional agreements with India and with Australia and New Zealand jointly. The organization has also discussed FTAs with the EU.

The varying degrees of intensity of FTA activity across economies in Asia can be related to factors including economic geography, economic size, per-capita income, levels of protection, and the production-network strategies of MNCs (Appendix Table 1).

Singapore is by far the most active Asian economy in terms of the number and geographic extent of FTAs. With its strategic location and world-class infrastructure and logistics, and as one of the region's most open economies, Singapore is the regional headquarters for many leading MNCs and regional organizations (e.g., the ASEAN+3 Macroeconomic Research Office [AMRO], the APEC Secretariat, and the International Secretariat of the Pacific Economic Cooperation Council [PECC]).

Singapore actively seeks access to new overseas markets, particularly for services and investments. The economy is a founding member of AFTA and has implemented bilateral agreements with the largest

Asian economies—China, India, Japan, and South Korea—as well as economies outside the region including Australia and the United States. The US-Singapore FTA, which has been in effect since 2004, was the first such agreement made in Asia by the United States and is reputed to be a model agreement in terms of scope (Koh and Lin 2004). Interestingly, the US approach to FTAs with ASEAN economies under the "Enterprise for ASEAN Initiative" expressly used the US-Singapore FTA as a model.

Despite being a supporter of multilateralism led by the WTO, Japan was a latecomer to FTAs (Urata 2004, Kawai and Urata 2012). The region's first developed economy has the strongest base of giant MNCs involved in production networks and supply chains throughout Asia. One motivation for Japan's engagement in FTAs is to provide a market-friendly and predictable regional business environment for its MNCs. Japan has rapidly implemented bilateral economic partnership agreements (EPAs) with 11 economies,[6] a regional agreement with ASEAN, and, in 2011, signed an EPA with Peru. More FTAs are expected in the future as Japan is negotiating agreements with Australia and the Gulf Cooperation Council economies, is exploring joining the on-going TPP negotiations, and has recently (May 2012) agreed to negotiations on a trilateral agreement with China and South Korea.

The two giant Asian developing economies, China and India, are forming FTAs to ensure market access for goods and to expand regional coverage for outward investment (Wignaraja 2011 and 2012b).

China implemented separate FTAs on goods and services with ASEAN and is now finalizing negotiations on an investment agreement. China has also forged bilateral comprehensive economic partnership agreements (CEPAs) with Hong Kong and Macau (Special Administrative Region, China); FTAs with Chile, Costa Rica, Pakistan, and Peru; and is a member of APTA. In addition, China concluded FTAs with New Zealand and Singapore in 2008 and an Economic Cooperation Framework Agreement with Taiwan in 2010.

India is also a member of APTA and, as a part of its "Look East" policy, has implemented several comprehensive agreements with East Asian economies (including ASEAN, Japan, Malaysia, Singapore, and South Korea) since 2005. It also has agreements with its South Asian neighbors.

Middle-income economies such as Malaysia and Thailand have emerged as regional production hubs for the electronics and auto industries, respectively. Malaysia is a participant in ASEANs' FTAs and has separate agreements with Chile, Japan, New Zealand, and Pakistan. Thailand, one of the founding members of ASEAN, has entered into bilateral agreements with Australia, China, India, Japan, and New Zealand. It also concluded an FTA with Peru in 2011.

Though South Korea does not have as many FTAs as other large economies in the region, it has strategically forged FTAs with the world's major traders (Europe and the United States) as well as ASEAN. Specifically, within Asia, South Korea has agreements with members of APTA, ASEAN, and Singapore. Outside Asia, South Korea has agreements with Chile and Peru and the EU and European Free Trade Area (EFTA) economies. The South Korea–US FTA was signed in June 2007 and took effect on 15 March 2012. The South Korea–EU FTA was signed in October 2010 and has been in force since July 2011.

With some exceptions, the region's lower-income economies—Cambodia, Indonesia, Lao PDR, Philippines, and Vietnam—have tended to rely on ASEAN for concluding FTAs with the region's larger economies. This may reflect a lack of human and technical resources, limited leverage, or a weak institutional capacity to undertake FTA negotiations. The ASEAN framework has allowed these economies to pool scarce capacity and resources.

The geographical orientation of Asian FTAs is summarized in Figure 3. A high degree of cross-regional orientation among some of the region's stronger economies—notably China, India, Singapore, and South Korea—is visible. The trend toward Asian cross-regional FTAs is even more evident in additional FTAs proposed and under negotiation. Asian economies are demonstrating their intent to open trading relations with the rest of the world rather than simply maintaining a regional focus (Kawai 2005).

Asian economies are demonstrating their intent to open trading relations with the world

A recent area of cross-regional expansion is Asia–Latin America economic ties. Driven by differences in demand, endowments, trade policies, and the emergence of large new economies, Asia–Latin

Figure 3. Geographical Orientation and Share of Concluded FTAs in Asia—FTAs within Asia and Cross-Regionally, 2012 (Number of FTAs by Economy)

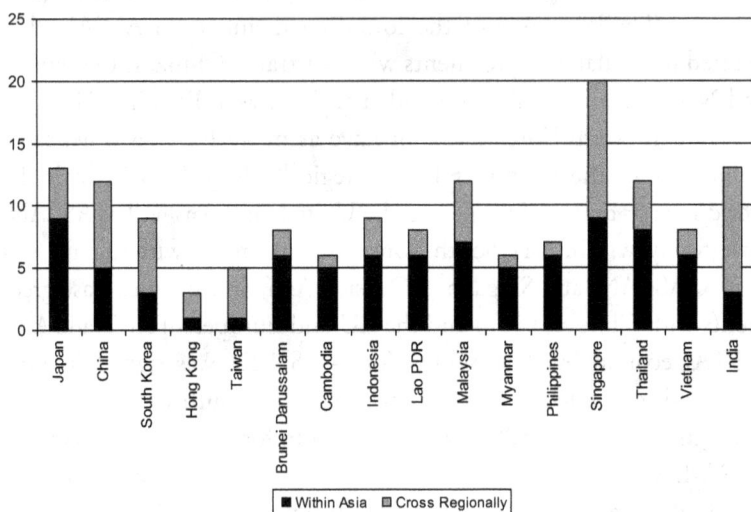

Source: ADB ARIC FTA Database (www.aric.adb.org; data as of September 2012).
Note: FTAs within Asia cover FTAs where all partners are in Asia. Here Asia includes the 16 economies listed in the figure.

America economic ties have grown rapidly since 2000 (ADB, IDB, and ADBI 2012). The slowdown in industrial economies following the global financial crisis may have also contributed to growing South-South investment and trade. Market-led integration has been followed by FTAs.

Since the first Asia–Latin America FTA emerged in 2004, an average of two FTAs have taken effect every year between economies of the two regions. As of 2012 there were 20 such agreements in effect (Wignaraja, Ramizo, and Burmeister 2012). This figure is projected to rise to 30 by 2020.

This growth in cross-regional FTAs has been led by the major trading economies from the two regions. Key agreements include the India-Chile FTA, the Japan-Mexico EPA, the South Korea–Chile FTA, and the China–Costa Rica FTA. ASEAN and other South Asian economies do not trade much with Latin American economies and have not participated in many cross-regional FTAs.

Future agenda-sustaining Asia–Latin America economic ties include emphasizing deep-integration FTAs, increasing the number of economies involved, promoting inter-regional investment, and pursuing domestic structural reforms. Effective partnerships among businesses, governments, and regional institutions will facilitate these ambitious goals.

Trade Coverage of Asian FTAs

The number of Asian FTAs concluded over a given time is relatively easy to track. However the numbers alone fail to indicate the economy-level importance of FTAs to economic activity or trade.

While difficult to measure because of the numerous exceptions and exclusions contained in many agreements, it would be valuable to generate some estimate of how much of an Asian economy's world trade is covered by FTA provisions.[7] Official statistics on utilization rates of Asian FTA preferences are difficult to obtain and no published data on the direction of services trade exist.

Only by making the bold assumption that all currently existing Asian trade in goods is covered by concluded FTAs may generally indicative estimates be obtained.[8] Working from this assumption, Figure 4 and Appendix Table 1 attempt to show the share of an economy's bilateral trade with its FTA partners as an element of its total world trade for 2000 and 2010. Figures for the EU and the United States are also reported.

Two observations may be made:

First, the region's larger economies have smaller relative shares in 2010 than do ASEAN member economies, highlighting the latter's greater reliance on FTAs (especially AFTA). In descending order, the shares for the larger economies are: South Korea (42 percent), China (27 percent), India (23 percent), and Japan (11 percent). ASEAN member economies display significant diversity with Brunei Darussalam, Lao PDR, and Myanmar having shares in excess of 80 percent and Indonesia and Singapore over 65 percent. Other ASEAN economies range between 62 percent and 51 percent.[9] Taiwan has the lowest noted share, at 15 percent, of its world trade covered by FTAs.

Second, reflecting the spread of FTAs throughout the region, all noted Asian economies experienced a significant increase in reliance on FTAs between 2000 and 2010. Asia's largest economies—China,

Figure 4. Share of an Economy's Trade with its FTA Partners Relative to the Economy's Trade with the World— 2000 and 2010 (by Percent of Total Trade)

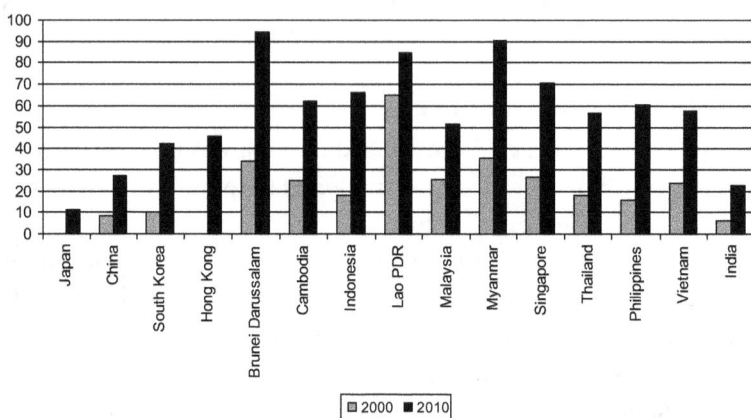

Sources: ADB staff estimates based on *Direction of Trade Statistics*, International Monetary Fund (data as of November 2009) and ADB ARIC FTA database (www. aric.adb.org; data as of September 2012).

Note: Data only covers FTAs concluded for the noted year. Hong Kong and Japan had no FTA partners in 2000.

India, Japan, and South Korea—have experienced at least a quadrupling of the ratio of trade covered by FTAs to total world trade over this period. Notable increases are also visible in most ASEAN economies.

It is interesting to compare the current trade coverage of FTAs in Asia's largest economies with those of the EU (34 percent)[10] and the United States (26 percent). The South Korean economy's trade coverage exceeds that of the EU and the United States while the Chinese economy's trade coverage exceeds that of the United States. The trade coverage of the economies of India and Japan are below those of the EU and the United States.

Challenges Posed by Asian Free Trade Agreements

As FTAs have spread across Asia concerns over such agreements have increased (Baldwin 2006, Tumbarello 2007, World Bank 2007, Bhagwati 2008, Drysdale and Armstrong 2010, Hoekman and Mattoo 2011). A cursory analysis of the growing number of conference reports, media stories, policy studies, and political debates concerning Asian FTAs indicates numerous challenges existing for regional integration.

This study is not intended to address the myriad economic, legal, and political issues arising from increasing Asian trade integration.

This study pragmatically examines patterns and challenges in Asian FTAs with a view to offering policy guidance. In particular, six key challenges associated with Asian FTAs merit further examination: 1) increasing enterprise-level use of FTAs, 2) tackling the Asian noodle bowl problem, 3) promoting comprehensive coverage of agricultural trade, 4) facilitating services-trade liberalization, 5) increasing WTO-plus elements, and 6) forming a region-wide FTA.

New evidence from enterprise-level surveys, analysis of agreements, and CGE models may be useful in analyzing some of these challenges and offering possible options for future actions.

Challenge 1: Increasing Use of FTA Preferences

Increasing the actual use of FTA preferences at the enterprise level may be the most critical challenge associated with Asian FTAs. Well designed and comprehensive FTAs offer numerous enterprise-level benefits including market access, new business opportunities, and preferential tariffs.

It might appear reasonable to assume that enterprises would actively avail themselves of such benefits once an appropriate FTA was in effect. Previous studies at both the economy and industry levels, however, suggest that FTA preference utilization rates—based on shares of export value enjoying preferences— are low in Asian economies and that such FTAs are underutilized (Baldwin 2006, World Bank 2007, Drysdale and Armstrong 2010). A enterprise-level study of Japan's FTAs also reported modest preference utilization rates and related this to the low volume of trade with FTA partner economies (Takahashi and Urata 2008). Accordingly, in developing Asian economies FTAs are often viewed as discriminatory and an unwanted drain on scarce trade-negotiation capacities (Bhagwati 2008).

> *Studies suggest that FTA preference utilization rates are low in Asian countries and that such FTAs are underutilized*

Certificate-of-origin information drawn from customs authorities' or business associations' databases comprehensively cover all users of FTA preferences within a given economy. Unfortunately one of the difficulties in investigating the evolution of Asian FTA preferences is that the significant majority of these economies do not publish such official information.

Fortunately Thailand is an exception and does publish (in the Thai language) official FTA-use data. This data was obtained from secondary sources (Chirathivat 2008, Udomwichaiwat 2012). Data for Vietnam is not published but was also available from a secondary source (Tran 2012). The available data from secondary sources suggest that FTA use has risen significantly in both Thailand and Vietnam. Strikingly, overall reported FTA use by enterprises in Thailand more than doubled from 27 percent in 2008 to 61 percent in 2011 (Chirathivat 2008, Udomwichaiwat 2012).

Appendix Table 2 provides a breakdown of FTA use for different agreements by Thailand and Vietnam.

Two of the findings shown for Thailand are especially noteworthy.

First, particularly high usage of trading preferences was shown for Thailand's bilateral and regional FTAs with its major trading partners in Asia and the Pacific in 2011. The Thailand-Australia FTA showed the greatest usage (91 percent) followed by that of the ASEAN-China FTA (84 percent), the Thailand-India FTA (75 percent), and the Japan-Thailand EPA (71 percent). Meanwhile the AFTA showed usage at a reasonable 52 percent and the ASEAN–South Korea FTA at 59 percent. Substantially less (27 percent) use was made of the ASEAN-Australia-New Zealand FTA.

Second, where both regional and bilateral agreements exist with the same trading partner, the bilateral agreement appears to be more heavily used. Use of the Japan-Thailand EPA (71 percent) is much higher than that for the Japan-Thailand FTA (4 percent). Likewise, use of the Thailand-Australia FTA (91 percent) is higher than that of the ASEAN-Australia-New Zealand FTA (27 percent). More attractive tariff preferences for key products and simplified rules of origin (ROO) may explain why bilateral FTAs are more attractive to enterprises than regional agreements.

Vietnam shows a lower FTA use than Thailand. However, significantly, the Vietnamese figures have nearly trebled from 11 percent in 2008 to 31 percent in 2011 (Tran 2012). The growth in FTA use appears largely to be linked to trade with Japan and South Korea. In 2011 Vietnamese enterprises made particularly high use of the ASEAN–South Korea FTA (91 percent) and reasonable use of the ASEAN-Japan FTA (31 percent). Significantly lower use was made of the ASEAN-China FTA and AFTA (20 percent).

How does FTA use by Thailand and Vietnam compare with the use of seemingly similar FTAs in other regions?

For comparison, between 1998 and 2003 about 54 percent of all Canadian exports to the US made use of NAFTA preferences (Kunimoto and Sawchuk 2005). Encouragingly, the 2011 Thai average usage figure is higher than the Canadian average usage figure—however the Vietnamese usage figure is lower than this reference.

An important priority for future research on Asian economic regionalism will be to assemble and maintain a comprehensive dataset on FTA use by the area's individual economies.

While economy-level FTA use is available from certificate-of-origin data, such data do not clearly identify enterprise-level characteristics of FTA users nor enterprise-level impediments to FTA use. Greater micro-level analysis, using enterprise-level surveys, will be required to detect such issues in specific economies. Multi-economy enterprise-level survey studies are both expensive and time consuming but, when well done, such surveys can provide valuable economic and business insights.

Six comprehensive surveys of manufacturing exporting enterprises conducted in 2007–2008 by the ADB, the Asian Development Bank Institute (ADBI), and partner researchers in China, Japan, Philippines, Singapore, South Korea, and Thailand shed light on the use of FTA preferences (Kawai and Wignaraja 2011b, Wignaraja 2010). An additional survey of Malaysian FTA use was conducted by ADB and ADBI in 2012. Details of the enterprise-level survey methodology are provided in Kawai and Wignaraja (2011b).

Basically, teams of experienced researchers used a consistent questionnaire and random-sampling methods to

Enterprises surveyed included foreign and local ownership and large and small- and medium-sized enterprises

collect enterprise-level data. The enterprises surveyed in each economy included a mix of both foreign and local ownership and large enterprises and small- and medium-sized enterprises (SMEs). Enterprises were selected to be broadly representative of the local industries. The enterprises were drawn from the region's largest industries (e.g., automotive, electronics, garments, and textiles) as well as, in each economy, industries of specifically local significance (e.g., food in the Philippines and metals and machinery in South Korea).

Data on the percentage value of exports utilizing FTA preferences were not available from the enterprise-level surveys. However it was possible to estimate utilization of FTA preferences based on the incidence of enterprises—i.e., the share of sample enterprises in a given economy—that use FTA preferences. While such a proxy is not ideal, it is believed to be reasonably accurate.

In Thailand, for example, the utilization rate of FTAs based on certificates of origin matched well with the utilization rate found in the enterprise-level Thai survey. The enterprise-level Thai survey utilization rate of 25 percent closely approximates that of the 2008 figure of 27 percent provided by Chirathivat (2008) working from certificate-of-origin data from Thailand's Ministry of Commerce.

As discussed below, enterprise-level survey data confirm earlier findings obtained from certificate-of-origin data from two Asian economies that use of FTAs appears to be higher than expected from previous studies.

Figure 5 shows this measure for enterprises that use and plan to use FTAs. Asian exporting enterprises tend to utilize FTA preferences more frequently than previously thought and may even be increasing their utilization rate. Of the 1,075 Asian sample enterprises, 32.1 percent currently use FTA preferences. When plans for using FTA preferences are also factored in, 52.1 percent of all Asian enterprises either use or plan to use FTA preferences.

These figures seem reasonable given the low applied MFN tariffs (averaging 7.4 percent in 2010) for the region. Japanese and Chinese enterprises are the highest users of FTA preferences while enterprises from Malaysia, Philippines, Singapore, South Korea, and Thailand make relatively less use of such preferences. Enterprises in all seven economies—but particularly China, Japan, Malaysia, and South Korea—have plans in place to increase their use of FTA preferences.

Figure 5. Utilization of FTA Preferences
(by Percent of Respondents by Economy)

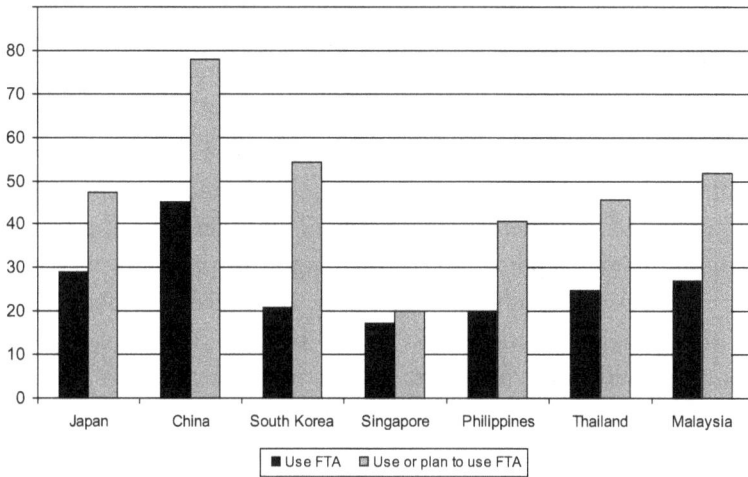

Source: Kawai and Wignaraja (2011b), ADB/ADBI Malaysia FTA Survey in 2012.

While these findings are encouraging, room for improvement at the enterprise level clearly exists in Asian use of FTA preferences.

T-tests (which assess whether the means of two groups are statistically different from each other) indicate that a key difference between those Asian enterprises using FTA preferences and those Asian enterprises not using FTA preferences is in enterprise size.

Japan is noteworthy for the number and scale of its large multinational corporations.

Japanese enterprises using FTA preferences average 30,104 employees. The equivalent number for China is 3,542 employees, for Singapore it is 1,098 employees, for Thailand it is 591 employees, for Malaysia it is 404 employees, and for the Philippines it is 395 employees.

Japanese enterprises *not* using FTA preferences average 7,020 employees. The equivalent number for China is 2,226 employees, for Thailand it is 291 employees, for the Philippines it is 269 employees, for Singapore it is 142 employees, and for Malaysia it is 86 employees.

Enterprise size clearly appears to underlie the pattern of FTA-preference use in the Asian sample. The results suggest that using FTAs entails significant fixed costs—e.g., learning about FTA provisions, tailoring business plans to complex tariff schedules, and obtaining certificates of origin—and larger enterprises are better able to muster the requisite financial and human resources than SMEs.

Reasons that the majority of the sampled Asian enterprises do not currently use FTA preferences are not clearly identified—however the ADB surveys did generate responses from 717 sampled Asian enterprises.

Perhaps surprisingly, a lack of information on FTAs was the most common reason cited for non-use of FTA preferences as reported by 39 percent of the enterprises surveyed. The second and third most common reasons reported were low margins of preference (15 percent) and delays and administrative costs associated with documenting and complying with the ROO (13 percent). Other reasons for non-use included: the use of other programs such as export processing zones and Information Technology Agreement(s) for exporters which provide alternative incentives (7 percent) and non-tariff measures in partner economies that inhibit imports and, hence, inhibit the use of FTA preferences (5 percent).

From these responses it would appear that the use of FTA preferences may be encouraged by: 1) raising awareness of FTA provisions, including the phasing out of tariff schedules; 2) increasing the margins of preferences at the product level; and 3) easing administrative procedures for documentation of and compliance with ROO.

Business associations and individual economies could make information on how to use FTAs, particularly for SMEs, more transparent. Practical ideas include frequent seminars with SMEs, television programs directed at businesses, and dedicated websites and telephone help lines. More generally, institutional support systems for businesses, particularly for SMEs, need to be improved. Existing support systems for exporting under FTAs vary greatly in their quality and frequency of usage.

Significant public and private investment is required in Asia to improve the coverage of support services, upgrade service quality, and reduce bureaucratic impediments. Business and industry associations have to play a greater role in providing members with support services for FTA exporting. Upgrading SME productivity, quality, and technical standards would aid their greater participation in regional production networks driven by large enterprises.

Lastly, a region-wide database on FTA use should be established and maintained so that FTA use may be continuously tracked.

Challenge 2: Tackling the Asian Noodle Bowl

As noted above, ROO requirements pose a significant challenge in increasing the usage of Asian FTAs. ROO are used to determine which goods enjoy preferential tariffs to prevent trade deflection among FTA members.

For manufactured goods, ROO address three issues: 1) changes in tariff-classification rules defined by detailed harmonized systems; 2) local (or regional)-value content rules requiring products to satisfy minimum local (or regional) values in the economy (or region) of the FTA; and 3) specific process rules requiring specific production processes (Estevadeordal and Suominen 2006).

Influential technical literature has argued that Asian FTAs have overly complicated ROO, initiating concerns that these rules and administrative procedures add unreasonably to costs of doing business (Manchin and Pelkmans-Balaoing 2007, Tumbarello 2007). Such literature argues that excessively restrictive and complex ROO in Asian FTAs deter the use of FTA preferences and raise enterprise transactions costs. This literature further suggests that, with the rapid spread of FTAs throughout Asia, multiple ROO in overlapping FTAs pose a severe burden for SMEs which have less ability to meet such costs.

> *Some literature has argued that Asian FTAs have overly complicated rules of origin*

Originally termed a "spaghetti bowl" of trade deals (Bhagwati 1995), this phenomenon has become widely known in Asia as the noodle bowl effect.[11]

To what extent are multiple ROO actually perceived as problematic by Asian enterprises? The ADB enterprise-level surveys provide interesting insights (Kawai and Wignaraja 2011b) into this issue. The ADB surveys (addressed below) provide enterprise-level perceptions of whether dealing with multiple ROO in the region's FTAs significantly add to business costs.

First, given the present level of concluded FTAs in the region, evidence suggests that multiple ROO impose only a limited burden on

Asian enterprises. Of the 922 enterprises responding to this concern, only 197 (21.4 percent) said that multiple ROO significantly add to business costs. The majority of the sampled enterprises did not presently find multiple ROO a problem.

The aggregate figure, however, masks interesting economy-level variations. Singaporean enterprises had the most (38 percent) negative perceptions regarding multiple ROO while Chinese enterprises had the least (6 percent). Between these extremes of negative responses, in descending order, were Japanese (31 percent), Philippine (28 percent), Thai (26 percent), Malaysian (25 percent), and South Korean (15 percent) enterprises. Economy-level FTA strategies, industrial structures, and the quality of institutional support may underlie differences in perceptions of ROO across Asian economies.

Second, the surveys unexpectedly found that larger Asian enterprises had greater negative perceptions of multiple ROO than did SMEs (Figure 6).

This relationship between enterprise size and concerns about multiple ROO presented an interesting research puzzle. Econometric analysis showed that large established enterprises tend to export to multiple markets and adjust their business plans in response to FTAs. They are, therefore, more likely to complain about issues of multiple ROO (Kawai and Wignaraja 2009b). Smaller enterprises, in contrast, tend to export to a single market and hence do not have much basis for complaining. While inter-economy and intra-enterprise size variations exist, little variation in perception across sectors was identified.

Third, the majority of surveyed enterprises would prefer to be able to select the specific ROO included in FTAs. The surveys suggest that enterprises are supportive of having alternative ROO for the same product: 1) if they cannot reach the value-content requirement, having alternative ROO might enable enterprises to still make use of FTA preferences; 2) as applications using the value-content rule often require confidential cost information, many suppliers and enterprises are reluctant to divulge such information; and 3) particular ROO are frequently aligned with the technology and production process of particular industries and are less pertinent to all others.

The general finding of limited burdens imposed by multiple ROO does not mean that policymakers should be complacent on this topic.

Figure 6. Burden Imposed by Multiple Rules of Origin in FTAs (by Percent of Respondents by Enterprise Size)

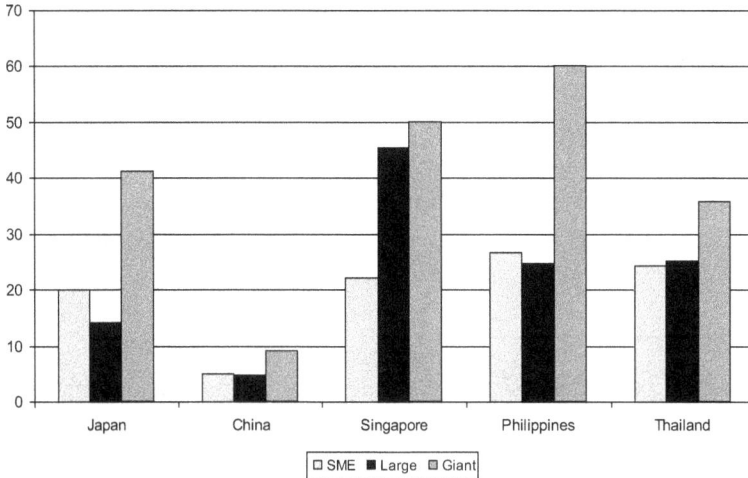

Source: Kawai and Wignaraja (2011b).
Note: SME (small- and medium-sized enterprise) = 100 or fewer employees
Large (enterprise) = 101 to 1,000 employees
Giant (enterprise) = more than 1,000 employees.

As the number of concluded agreements increases, multiple ROO may well become more of a problem for more enterprises. Supportive measures—such as encouraging rationalization of ROO and upgrading their administration—are needed to mitigate the future negative effects of the Asian noodle bowl.

Widespread gains in Asian economies are possible from pursuing simplified approaches to ROO. These would involve harmonizing ROO, addressing the accumulation of value content, and coequality of ROO.[12] It would be extremely useful to identify and adopt international best practices in ROO administration. Such practices might include introducing a trusted-trader program (as used in NAFTA) allowing successful applicants to self-certify their own certificates of origin, allowing business associations to issue fee-based certificates of origin, increasing the use of information technology-based systems of ROO administration, and better training of SMEs to enhance their capacity to use FTAs.

Challenge 3: Promoting Comprehensive Coverage of Agricultural Trade
A third challenge for Asian FTAs is extending the coverage of trade
in agricultural products. Existing literature suggests that FTA coverage of agricultural trade differs markedly among Asian economies.
In some cases agricultural products have been largely excluded from
FTA benefits because of pressures from powerful farm lobbies or,
where poverty is predominant in developing economies, social concerns over the rural sector (Feridhanusetyawan 2005).

Since 2000 the big push for Asian FTAs has addressed production networks in manufacturing. As production networks are not
particularly active in agriculture this may also be another cause
for the substantial exclusion of
agricultural trade. There is an
identifiable less-than-optimal level
of liberalization in trade in agricultural products. This conflicts
with the spirit of GATT article
XXIV addressing exemptions to
the WTO's most-favored-nation
or nondiscriminatory-treatment clause (Cheong and Cho, 2006).
GATT article XXIV requires FTAs to eliminate trade barriers within
a reasonable period of time on "substantially all trade" in originating
goods from members. This has been referred to as the "substantially
all trade" rule.

*The challenge for Asian FTAs
is extending the coverage of
trade in agricultural products*

Two issues have hampered empirical research on the Asian FTA
coverage of trade in agricultural products. First, little systematic data
and analysis are available on the treatment of agricultural products
across Asian FTAs. Second, clear criteria for the "substantially all
trade" rule do not seem to exist. With the development of new databases on Asian FTAs—e.g., ADB's Asia Regional Integration Center
database—new sources of FTA data are now available. Tariff lines for
agricultural products may now begin to be used as a basis to gauge
the criteria of "substantially all trade."

A simple three-level classification system was used to categorize
Asian FTAs according to tariff-line coverage of agricultural products.
Given the complexity of provisions for agriculture in many agreements, and the availability of tariff schedules and exclusion lists at
the product level, a combination of coverage of product lines and

exclusions was used to assess each agreement. Classifications were determined as follows:

1) Comprehensive coverage—at least 85 percent of all agricultural product lines in a given agreement are covered or not more than 150 product lines are excluded. FTAs with these features for agricultural products are taken as covering substantially all trade.
2) Some coverage—more agricultural products are included in FTAs than "little or no coverage," but fewer products are covered than in "comprehensive coverage." Agreements with some coverage typically include more than 100 agricultural product lines but less than 85 percent of agricultural product lines. These agreements may also exclude over 150 agricultural product lines.
3) Little or no coverage—less than 100 product lines are included or agricultural products are completely excluded from the agreement.

It was possible to apply this classification system to the agricultural coverage of Asian FTAs concluded between 2000 and 2012 (Figure 7). The data suggest that, over time, Asian FTAs are becoming more comprehensive in their coverage of agricultural products.

AFTA, for instance, was originally proposed to address only ten manufacturing sectors but was later expanded to included agricultural products. The three Asian FTAs concluded in 2000 had little or no coverage of agriculture. By 2005 the number of Asian FTAs concluded grew to 22. Of these eight (36 percent) were regarded as comprehensive in their coverage of agricultural products, five (23 percent) had some coverage, and nine (41 percent) had little or no coverage.

Since 2005 the number of concluded Asian FTAs has continued to increase. As of September 2012, texts were available for 69 FTAs.[13] Of these, 32 (46 percent) are comprehensive in their coverage of agricultural products, 19 (28 percent) had some coverage, and 18 (26 percent) had little or no coverage.

South Korean FTAs provide the most comprehensive coverage of agricultural products. Upon entry into force, the South Korea–US FTA will eliminate tariffs on almost two-thirds of current US

Figure 7. Agricultural Coverage of Asian FTAs, 2000–2012
(Number of FTAs)

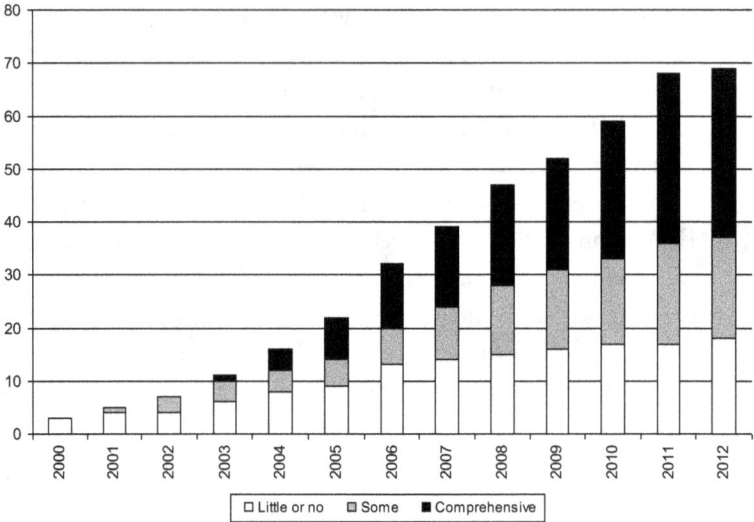

Source: Legal annexes of FTAs (www.aric.adb.org) and WTO reports; data as of September 2012.

Notes: 1) The data cover only 69 Asian FTAs because online official texts for two FTAs were unavailable. Agricultural products and chapters are classified according to World Trade Organization (WTO) classification.

2) Comprehensive coverage—at least 85 percent of all agricultural product lines in a given agreement are covered or not more than 150 product lines are excluded.

Some coverage—more agricultural products are included in FTAs than "little or no coverage," but less products are covered than in "comprehensive coverage." Agreements with some coverage typically include more than 100 agricultural product lines but less than 85 percent of agricultural product lines. These agreements may also exclude over 150 agricultural product lines.

Little or no coverage—less than 100 product lines are included or agricultural products are completely excluded from the agreement.

agricultural exports including corn, cotton, and wheat. Tariffs and import quotas on most other agricultural products will be phased out within 10 years. South Korea even agreed to eliminate its 40 percent tariff on beef muscle meats over a 15-year period.[14] The South Korea–Chile FTA is taken as a comprehensive agreement for agricultural products as South Korea excludes only 21 agricultural products, such as apples, pears, and rice, from the agreement. These exclusions are likely because of a lack of seasonal competition.

Three of Japan's FTAs (with India, Philippines, and Vietnam) have comprehensive coverage of agricultural products while the rest have some coverage. Under the Japan-Vietnam FTA that took effect in 2009, Japan immediately eliminated 784 out of 2,020 tariff lines on farm products addressing 67.6 percent of Vietnam's total agricultural product export value to Japan. Japan committed to cut tariffs on 86 percent of agricultural, aquatic, and forestry exports from Vietnam within 10 years from the effective date of the agreement.

AFTA is also regarded as a comprehensive agreement as, on average, members exclude only 20 agricultural products.[15]

The ASEAN-Australia-New Zealand FTA follows the AFTA model where most tariffs on agricultural products are either eliminated upon the FTA's entry into force or are to be eliminated by 2020. Exclusions from tariff commitments, including maize, rice, and sugar, have been kept to a minimum. ASEAN economies have liberalized key export sectors for Australia including dairy, fish, grains, and meat. Specifically, most meat tariffs are eliminated upon entry in force of the FTA or will be phased out over time while only a few meat tariffs, in a few economies, remain untouched.

While China's early FTAs tended to have little coverage of agricultural products, more recent agreements have placed more emphasis on this sector. Today China has five FTAs with comprehensive coverage of agricultural products and another two with some coverage. The China–New Zealand FTA is a benchmark FTA with comprehensive coverage as tariffs on most key New Zealand agricultural products will be phased out by 2019. This

The China–New Zealand FTA is a benchmark with comprehensive coverage of agricultural products

includes tariffs on apples (2012), beef and sheep (2016), all dairy products (by 2019), kiwifruit (2016), and seafood (2012). A special safeguard measure has been made available to China with regard to certain dairy products.

India similarly under-emphasized the coverage of agricultural products until recently. India's three FTAs with comprehensive coverage of agricultural products (with ASEAN, Japan, and South Korea) were concluded after 2009.

Criteria must be further refined for accurately assessing the coverage of agricultural products in Asian FTAs according to the "substantially all trade" rule. New criteria must also be developed to assess the value of total trade.

While more extensive coverage of agricultural trade by Asian FTAs is still needed, a gradual approach to liberalization seems optimal for developing economies. Agricultural products are a key element in the continuing liberalization of goods trade.

It will be important for all future FTAs to include provisions on agricultural products. This will drive producers to adjust to competition and improve productivity. FTAs meeting the benchmark for comprehensiveness by covering at least 85 percent of all agricultural product lines in a given agreement and minimizing exclusions to not more than 150 product lines should be recognized as the next step. This can be accomplished by adopting a "negative list approach"[16] to agricultural products in the drafting of new FTAs and allowing the exclusion of only a few sensitive items. Future issues include realistic tariff-elimination schedules, transparent sanitary and phytosanitary regimes, and subsidy reforms.

Challenge 4: Facilitating Services-Trade Liberalization

Facilitating services-trade liberalization is an ongoing challenge for Asian FTAs. Services account for more than half the GDP of most Asian economies and such trade is rapidly growing (Hoekman and Mattoo 2011). Impediments to trade in services, particularly regulatory restrictions on foreign services and service providers, exist across Asia (Findlay, Ochiai, and De 2009). These impediments involve licensing, ownership rules, qualification requirements, and/or technical regulations.

Largely because of limited efforts by governments and/or the private sectors, WTO multilateral negotiations on services trade have made little progress (Hoekman and Mattoo 2011). However services-trade liberalization would support increasing the growth in services trade and would improve the operation of production networks increasingly dependant on efficient logistics and trade facilitation.

Many current comprehensive FTAs seek to remove regulatory restrictions on services trade and the operation of services providers. Article V of the General Agreement on Trade in Services (GATS) requires WTO members to conclude FTAs that: 1) address substantial sectoral coverage (i.e., in terms of number of sectors, volume of trade affected, and modes of supply) ; 2) eliminate discrimination in the form of national treatment; and 3) do not raise barriers against nonmembers. Developing countries, however, have more flexibility in fulfilling conditions 1 and 2.

In practice it is difficult to assess conformity of an FTA with GATS Article V. Lack of services-trade data makes it difficult to estimate the value of the services trade covered by an FTA. There is little consensus on the meaning of "substantial sectoral coverage" in the services trade and assessments of "national treatment" require detailed subsectoral analysis. Varying enthusiasms (i.e., positive, mixed, and/or actively negative) to the liberalization of services trade in GATS negotiations and, particularly, the absence of disaggregated data on services trade makes it almost impossible to accurately quantify substantial sectoral coverage.

A practical answer is to focus on requirement (1) of GATS Article V and to interpret "substantial sectoral coverage" to mean that a high-quality FTA must cover key services sectors. This approach, drawing on Wignaraja and Lazaro (2010), can be readily applied to many Asian FTAs.[17] The GATS classification list of 12 service sectors is functional for creating a simple three-element services-trade classification of Asian FTAs:

1) Comprehensive coverage: The FTA covers the five key GATS sectors—business and professional services, communications services, financial services, transport services, and labor mobility/entry of business persons. Coverage of other sectors may also be included. These five sectors were chosen as references as they are the largest sectors in terms of the value of services trade in Asia and are also frequently subject to multiple regulatory barriers on foreign services and service providers.

2) Some coverage: The FTA would typically cover between two and four key GATS sectors and some minor GATS sectors.

3) Little or no coverage of services: The FTA either excludes services-trade liberalization or provides only general provisions therefore or covers only one of the five key GATS sectors and/or some minor GATS sectors.

A sector is considered covered if at least one party includes its GATS and GATS-plus (liberalizing services-trade policies beyond GATS commitments in relation to subsectors or regulations) commitments, regardless of the number of subsectors, volume of trade affected, or the four modes of supply.[18]

This classification system was applied to 2000–2012 Asian FTAs (Figure 8). The evidence indicates a trend in Asian FTAs towards progressively liberalizing the services-trade sectors of participants and providing, over time, for deeper regulatory cooperation in services trade.

In the early 2000s the majority of Asian FTAs had some or little coverage of services trade. By 2005, ten FTAs[19] (45 percent) were considered comprehensive in covering at least five key services, five (23 percent) provided coverage of between two and four key sectors, and seven (32 percent) had little or no coverage. Thereafter, most new FTAs typically incorporated either comprehensive or some coverage of services. Of the 69 FTAs extant in 2012, 28 (41 percent) were comprehensive and another 25 (36 percent) had some coverage. Only 16 (23 percent) had little or no coverage.

Many Asian FTAs adhere to such key GATS principles as market access (quota elimination); national treatment (equal treatment of local and foreign service providers); MFN treatment (service suppliers of an FTA member will automatically receive benefits given to other future FTA parties); reasonable, impartial, and objective domestic regulations; transparency; and mutual recognition agreements (MRAs). MRAs enable the qualifications of professional services suppliers to be mutually recognized by signatory members, thereby facilitating the easier movement of professional-services providers among the member economies.

> *Mutual recognition agreements facilitate the easier movement of professional-services providers*

Several Asian FTAs also provide for GATS-plus commitments meaning that the FTA liberalization of services-trade policies goes beyond WTO commitments in relation to subsectors or regulations.

The Japan-Singapore agreement is particularly comprehensive with each signatory expanding its commitments in more than 130 sectors focusing on national treatment (i.e., treating service suppliers

Figure 8. Services-trade Coverage of Asian FTAs, 2000–2012
(Number of FTAs)

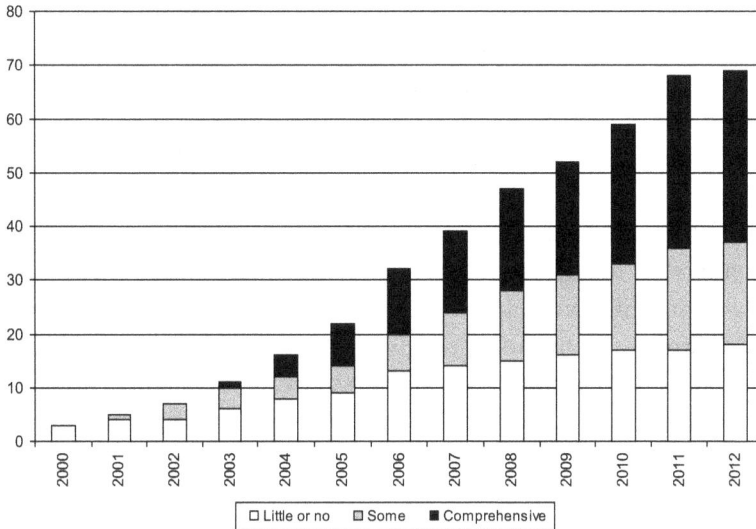

Source: Legal annexes of FTAs (www.aric.adb.org) and WTO reports; data as of September 2012.

Notes: 1) The data cover only 69 Asian FTAs because online official texts for two FTAs were unavailable.

2) Comprehensive coverage—includes the five key sectors of GATS: business and professional services, communications services, financial services, transport services, and labor mobility/entry of business persons.

Some coverage—typically covers between two and four key sectors of GATS and some minor sectors.

Little or no coverage—either excludes services-trade liberalization or provides only general provisions therefore or covers only one of the five key sectors and some minor sectors.

from the FTA partner economy as nationals). Additional comprehensive disciplines for financial and telecommunications services are imposed through two separate annexes. In the South Korea–EU FTA, South Korea commits to liberalize more than a hundred sectors, including construction, environmental, financial, postal and express delivery, professional services (e.g., accounting, architectural, engineering, and legal services), telecommunications, and transport. For example, in telecommunications South Korea will relax foreign ownership requirements, allowing 100 percent indirect ownership within two years of the entry into force of the agreement. Further,

EU shipping enterprises will gain full market access and the right of establishment in South Korea in addition to non-discriminatory treatment in the use of port services and infrastructure. Additionally, EU law firms will be allowed to open offices in South Korea to advise both foreign and domestic clients on non–South Korean law and lawyers will be allowed to use their domestic job titles (e.g., avocat or solicitor).

In the ASEAN-Australia-New Zealand FTA the five original ASEAN members (Indonesia, Malaysia, Philippines, Singapore, and Thailand) expanded the liberalization of their telecommunication services to additional subsectors, while four of them (Indonesia, Malaysia, Philippines, and Singapore) went even further with their commitments in financial services. Australia and New Zealand have also made GATS-plus commitments covering cross-border trade in services, consumption abroad, and commercial presence in multiple sectors including business and financial services.

Notable comprehensive coverage of services trade among other Asian FTAs include the ASEAN FTA, India-Singapore Comprehensive Economic Cooperation Agreement (CECA), and China-Singapore FTA.

ASEAN economies began to negotiate on services trade in 1995 through the ASEAN Framework Agreement on Services. To date, ASEAN has concluded at least seven packages of commitment, agreed on five priority services sectors (air transport, e-ASEAN, healthcare, logistics, and tourism), and seven MRAs. These include accounting, architectural, engineering, medical, dental, nursing, and surveying services. ASEAN is continuously negotiating all other sectors and modes of supply to achieve the free flow of services by 2015 in line with its blueprint for an ASEAN Economic Community.

Under the India-Singapore CECA, preferential treatment is given for all five of the major services sectors as well as for construction and related engineering, distribution, education, environmental, and tourism and travel-related services. The services-trade coverage of the China-Singapore FTA goes beyond GATS to incorporate commitments under the ASEAN-China FTA and also includes a chapter on the movement of natural persons.

While there continues to be variation across Asian FTAs in terms of coverage of services trade, more emphasis is now being placed on services-trade liberalization. Newer agreements, particularly those between developed and developing economies, typically encompass the five key sectors of GATS.

Radical liberalization of services trade via the WTO or Asian FTAs seems unlikely for political and economic reasons. With limited opportunity for multilateral service-trade liberalization, a modest way forward is for all future Asian FTAs to cover the five key sectors of GATS. Such coverage should adhere, at least, to GATS principles (such as market access, national treatment, transparency, and mutual recognition agreements) and contain only limited exemptions. Sectoral coverage may be extended over time and further GATS-plus commitments may be considered—particularly in agreements encompassing more-developed economies.

Challenge 5: Increasing WTO-Plus Elements

Asian FTAs must now be expanded to address issues beyond the original WTO framework. The WTO system that emerged from the Uruguay Round in the mid-1990s consisted of substantive agreements on goods and services. The subsequent WTO Doha Round trade talks initiated in 2001 have focused on liberalization in agricultural and non-agricultural market access. The four Singapore issues (competition, intellectual property, investment, and public procurement) were earlier conditionally included in the work program for the Doha Round trade talks but were dropped by the WTO Ministerial Conference in Cancun in 2004.

WTO-plus agreements and comprehensive "new age" FTAs— those addressing the Singapore issues—are becoming more common throughout the world (Fiorentino, Crawford, and Toqueboeuf 2009, Freund and Ornelas 2010). Increasing WTO-plus elements in Asian FTAs is recognized as a critical challenge for Asian economies. Existing studies show Asian FTAs vary considerably in their scope with some being highly sophisticated while others are more limited (Banda and Whalley 2005, Plummer 2007).[20] However a systematic cross-economy review of the

> *WTO-plus agreements and those addressing the Singapore issues are becoming more common throughout the world*

full scope of Asian FTAs remains lacking, particularly with regard to more recent agreements.

Figure 9 shows the scope of identified concluded Asian FTAs between 2000 and 2012 and Figure 10 shows these FTAs by economy for 2012 by: 1) narrow agreements that deal with goods and/or services; 2) somewhat broader agreements covering goods, services, and some Singapore issues (partial WTO-plus); and 3) comprehensive agreements covering goods, services, and all four Singapore issues (comprehensive WTO-plus). Those FTAs shown in categories 2) and 3) may be considered WTO-plus FTAs. The scope of concluded agreements reflects a combination of economic interests, economic strength, and negotiation capacity.

The pattern is striking. Early Asian FTAs seemed to be concerned largely with goods and services. From the mid-2000s onwards, however, significantly more emphasis was given to broad agreements with many WTO-plus elements (Figure 9). By 2012, 16 (23 percent) FTAs were goods and/or services only, 37 (54 percent) FTAs were

Figure 9. Scope of Concluded FTAs in Asia, 2000–2012 (Number of FTAs)

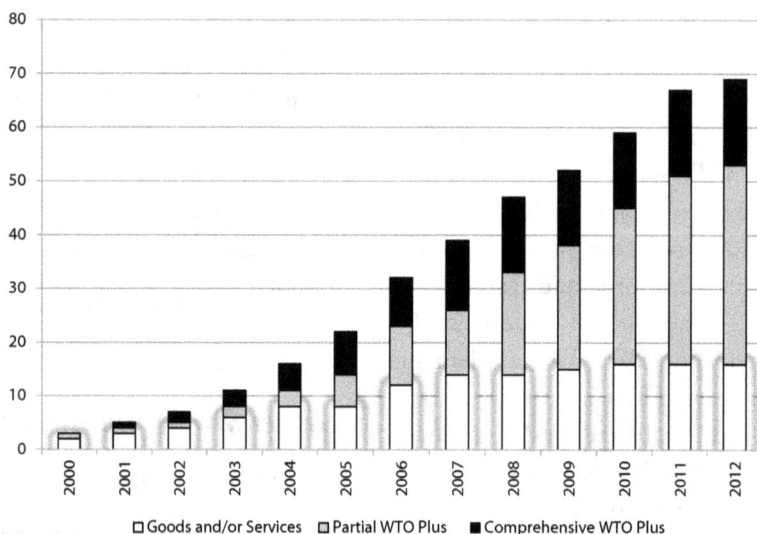

□ Goods and/or Services   □ Partial WTO Plus   ■ Comprehensive WTO Plus

Source: FTAs and ARIC FTA Database (www.aric.adb.org); data as of September 2012.
Note: The data cover only 69 Asian FTAs because online official texts for two FTAs were unavailable.

Figure 10. Scope of Concluded FTAs in Asia
(Number of FTAs with Narrow and WTO-plus Coverage
by Economy)

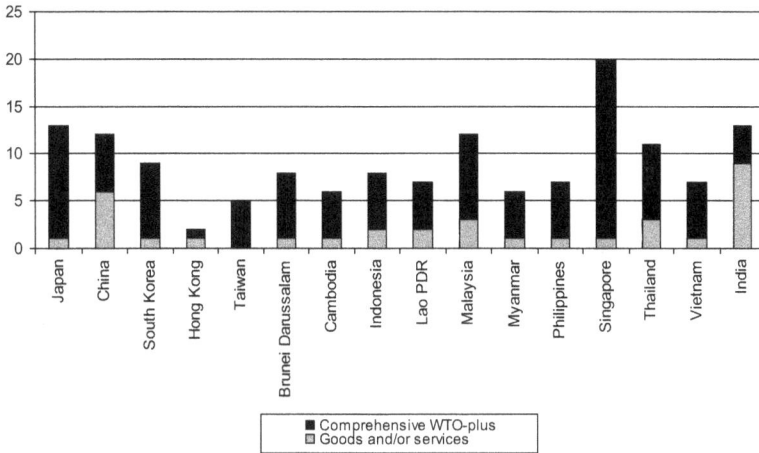

Source: ADB ARIC FTA Database (www.aric.adb.org); data as of September 2012.
Note: The data cover only 69 Asian FTAs because online official texts for two FTAs were unavailable.

partial WTO-plus, and 16 (23 percent) FTAs were comprehensive WTO-plus.

Three leading participants in Asian FTAs—Japan, Singapore, and South Korea—strongly favor the WTO-plus approach to FTAs and are increasingly emphasizing comprehensive agreements (Figure 10). Appendix Table 3 summarizes coverage of selected FTAs by participants. All of Japan's agreements and most of Singapore's and South Korea's are WTO-plus. Brunei Darussalam, Indonesia, Malaysia, Philippines, Thailand, and Vietnam FTAs also largely follow the WTO-plus format.

Historically China and India have been relatively cautious regarding the scope of their FTAs, preferring agreements focusing on goods and services elements. More recently, however, both economies have begun to experiment by incorporating some WTO-plus provisions into agreements such as the India-Singapore CECA, the Japan-India EPA, and the China–New Zealand FTA. Thus, with a few exceptions, Asian economies are increasingly favoring WTO-plus rather than narrowly limited agreements.

Kawai and Wignaraja (2009a) address some additional noteworthy points concerning WTO-plus provisions in Asian FTAs. Agreements between developed economies and developing and emerging economies have generally taken the WTO-plus format. Examples include the ASEAN-Japan FTA, China–New Zealand FTA, South Korea–EU FTA, South Korea–US FTA, and US-Singapore FTA. Also Singapore and South Korea tend to behave like developed economies in their agreements with many developing economies. This behavior is visible in the Transpacific Strategic EPA,[21] Singapore-China FTA, and South Korea–Chile FTA. Further, some existing FTAs are gradually being expanded to include WTO-plus coverage. Examples include the ASEAN–South Korea CEPA and the India–Sri Lanka CEPA. And finally, the trend towards increasing WTO-plus elements in Asian FTAs means that the region's FTA activity is likely to continue even if the Doha Round trade talks (focusing on liberalization in agricultural and non-agricultural market access) were to be concluded in the future.

The inclusion of WTO-plus provisions—particularly the four Singapore issues—would be desirable in all forthcoming Asian FTAs. The value of such efforts should be obvious. Competition policy and investment provisions are integral ingredients in facilitating FDI inflows and the development of production networks. Inclusion of provisions on trade facilitation and logistics development would help lower transactions costs in conducting trade. Cooperation provisions—along the line of the APEC Economic and Technical Cooperation (ECOTECH) agenda[22]—would stimulate technology transfer and industrial competitiveness.

In their FTA negotiations, the EU and the United States prefer a single agreement including such WTO-plus provisions. The South Korea–EU, South Korea–US, and US-Singapore agreements are cases in point. ASEAN is also considering an ASEAN Comprehensive Agreement on Investment as a part of moving toward an ASEAN Economic Community by 2015.

Challenge 6: Forming a Region-Wide FTA

There is increasing recognition in Asia of the merits of forming a region-wide FTA. Such an agreement would consolidate the existing plethora of bilateral and multilateral agreements. A region-wide

FTA would have multiple economic benefits: increased market access to goods, services, skills, and technology; increased market size permitting specialization and the realization of economies of scale; facilitating FDI and technology transfer by MNCs; and permitting simplification of rules, standards, and tariff schedules (Chia 2010).

ASEAN—with the region's oldest FTA—is emerging as an integration hub for Asian FTAs. China, Japan, and South Korea have all implemented FTAs with ASEAN. India and the combination of Australia and New Zealand are also implementing FTAs with ASEAN.

With key ASEAN+1 (ASEAN and one FTA partner) agreements underway, policy discussions in Asia are focusing on alternative region-wide FTA proposals—an East Asia Free Trade Area (EAFTA) among ASEAN+3 economies (the 10 ASEAN economies plus China, Japan, and South Korea) and a Comprehensive Economic Partnership for East Asia (CEPEA) among ASEAN+6 economies (the

A region-wide FTA would have multiple economic benefits

ASEAN+3 economies plus Australia, India, and New Zealand)— that will guide future policy-led integration in the region.

Seeking to bridge ASEAN and its Northeast Asian neighbors, EAFTA was an early version of a region-wide FTA. CEPEA has emerged through the realization that synergies could be gained by linking ASEAN+3 economies with Australia, India, and New Zealand. It will be important to identify whether EAFTA or CEPEA would prove more economically beneficial for participants addressing the global economy.

Using CGE models, studies have been conducted on the impact of prospective FTAs on Asian economies (Gilbert, Scollay, and Bora 2004; Bchir and Fouquin 2006; Plummer and Wignaraja 2006; Kawai and Zhai 2010). An advantage of using CGE models is that these models are based on consistent structural equations describing economic activity in each economy.

While there has been CGE analysis on EAFTA and some other alternatives, only limited CGE analysis has been done on CEPEA or on comparisons between EAFTA and CEPEA (Lee, Owen, and van der Mensbrugghe 2009). Such work tends to focus on FTAs involving goods only, while other Asian FTA coverages—e.g., services and trade facilitation—have been excluded. More recent work (e.g., Petri, Plummer, and Zhai 2011) provides CGE estimates for both EAFTA and TPP leading to a Free Trade Area of the Asia-Pacific (FTAAP).

Figure 11 shows the results of a CGE study of economies in Asia. The EAFTA scenario provides for free trade among the 10 ASEAN members, China, Japan, and South Korea. The CEPEA scenario broadens the EAFTA scenario to include Australia, India, and New Zealand.

Four CGE model features are especially noteworthy: 1) strong microeconomic foundations and detailed interactions among consumers, governments, and industries across the global economy; 2) medium- to long-term investment effects by allowing for trade to affect capital stocks through investment activities; 3) use of the Global Trade Analysis Project database (version 6.3) through to 2017, which projects trade and production patterns to represent a post–Uruguay Round world using the phase-out of the Agreement on Textiles and Clothing, the implementation of the remaining WTO commitments under the Doha Round trade talks, and enlargement of the EU to 27 members; and 4) a stylized FTA that includes goods, services, and some aspects of trade-cost reduction. The model's baseline is 2017 and the simulations show changes from this baseline. As the formation of a region-wide FTA may take time, setting up the model and dataset in this way provides for more realistic scenarios.

Three overall results may be highlighted from the CGE study in terms of percentage change from the 2017 baseline income: 1) a region-wide FTA, whether EAFTA or CEPEA, offers larger gains to world income than the current wave of bilateral and multilateral FTAs; 2) the CEPEA scenario, which is broader in terms of economy coverage, offers larger gains to the world as a whole in terms of total additional income (US$260 billion, measured in constant 2001 prices) than the EAFTA scenario; and 3) third parties outside either EAFTA or CEPEA lose little from being excluded from a region-wide agreement.[23]

Some interesting economy-level results in terms of percentage change from 2017 baseline income emerge from this study (Figure 11):

- For ASEAN's more dynamic members, projected gains are significant under the CEPEA scenario: Thailand (12.8 percent), Vietnam (7.6 percent), Malaysia (6.3 percent), and Singapore (5.4 percent).

Figure 11. Income Effects of Alternative Scenarios
Compared to 2017 Baseline
(by Percent Change in GDP by Economy)

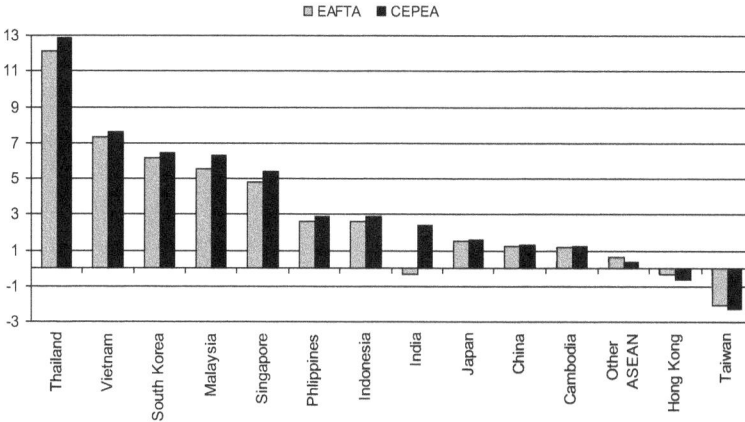

Source: Kawai and Wignaraja (2009a) based on the CGE model used in Francois and
Wignaraja (2008).
Notes: ASEAN = Association of Southeast Asian Nations
CEPEA = Comprehensive Economic Partnership for East Asia
EAFTA = East Asia Free Trade Area
GDP = gross domestic product.

- For the rest of ASEAN—Brunei Darussalam, Cambodia, Indonesia, Lao PDR, Myanmar, and Philippines—the gains are less than 3 percent.
- Among Northeast Asian economies, South Korea experiences the largest gain under EAFTA (6.2 percent) and CEPEA (6.4 percent) scenarios.
- Australia, India, and New Zealand experience losses under the EAFTA scenario and gains under the CEPEA scenario. The losses under EAFTA are less than 0.5 percent for each while under CEPEA gains are 3.9 percent for Australia, 2.4 percent for India, and 5.2 percent for New Zealand.
- Third parties such as Hong Kong and Taiwan experience small losses from being excluded from both EAFTA and CEPEA.

For the CEPEA scenario, Appendix Table 4 displays output effects across broad sectors compared to a projected 2017 baseline.

The implementation of the CEPEA scenario in Asia is likely to result in significant structural changes toward manufacturing and services (and away from agriculture and other primary products). There are also shifts within manufacturing. Among ASEAN's most dynamic members, Thailand witnesses projected gains in electrical machinery/electronics, motor vehicles, and services; Vietnam in clothing and textiles; and Malaysia in metals and metal products. Elsewhere in ASEAN, Cambodia sees losses in a key sector (clothing and textiles) and the Philippines sees losses in motor vehicles. China has gains in electrical machinery/electronics and India in metals and services. Japan and South Korea see gains in most manufacturing sectors. Strikingly, seven economies see declines in agriculture while the others see only negligible gains.

CGE analysis indicates that a region-wide agreement in East Asia—particularly CEPEA—provides welfare gains over the present wave of ASEAN+1 FTAs.[24] The gains to members of such an agreement are notable while losses to non-members are relatively small.

Thus arguments for and moves toward CEPEA are supported by economic modeling. The CGE analysis also reveals that some members gain more than others. This issue may need to be addressed in policy discussions. There is a case for further narrowing development gaps by providing financial and technical support for low-income economies. This is particularly true with respect to capacity building, customs modernization, enhancing SME development, governance reforms, and trade-related infrastructure.

> *Analysis indicates that a region-wide agreement provides welfare gains over the present ASEAN+1 FTAs*

Political-Economy Considerations of Asian Free Trade Agreements

Consolidation in Asia

Even if the consolidation of FTAs into a region-wide agreement—whether in the form of EAFTA among the ASEAN+3 economies or CEPEA among the ASEAN+6 economies—demonstrably yields large economic gains to Asia, the future remains unclear. Political-economy considerations may significantly affect the process on the ground.

For example, China has been a strong supporter of EAFTA while Japan has put more emphasis on CEPEA. Political rivalry over FTA leadership in Asia could be expected to hinder any such joint venture. However, in late 2012, China agreed to begin negotiations of a Regional Comprehensive Economic Partnership (RCEP) among the ASEAN+6 countries.

Given the role in Asia of the United States as a security anchor for many regional economies, one may argue that excluding the United States from the Asian-integration process is not politically viable. Large, mature European markets also suggest that many Asian economies should work more closely with Europe to expand investment and trade.

We consider three competing scenarios for consolidation of various Asian FTAs into a larger FTA: 1) an East Asia–wide FTA, particularly in the form of a RCEP; 2) a Free Trade Area of the Asia-Pacific (FTAAP) among APEC economies; and 3) a Free Trade Area of Asia and Europe (FTAAE) among the Asia-Europe Meeting economies.

An East Asia–wide FTA—in the form of a RCEP—addresses the noodle bowl problem among Asia's production network economies while FTAAP or FTAAE takes into account external markets as well. The idea of forming EAFTA or CEPEA has been on the official agenda of the ASEAN+3 leaders' process and East Asia Summit meetings. The ASEAN Summit in Cambodia in November 2012 agreed that RCEP negotiation be launched in early 2013 among the ASEAN member states and ASEAN's FTA partners.[25] In the same vein, FTAAP has been officially considered in the APEC leaders' process. However the idea of establishing FTAAE has not yet attracted much political attention.

To discuss these scenarios and their feasibilities, some political-economic considerations have to be addressed with regard to an East Asia–wide FTA (EAFTA or CEPEA) and/or FTAAP.

Building Blocks for Wider Agreements
With the rise in the number of participants officially negotiating FTAs, creating an all-encompassing FTA for Asia and beyond could

become exceedingly complicated. This suggests that forming RCEP would be more complex than forming ASEAN+1 FTAs and that forming FTAAP would be even more complex.

A first step toward the consolidation of various FTAs might be to develop preliminary steps—building blocks—for a region-wide FTA (such as RCEP) and then to further develop additional steps leading to a trans-regional FTA (such as FTAAP and/or FTAAE).

ASEAN could act as Asia's integration hub or convener in forming an Asia-wide FTA and the "plus-six" economies—Australia, China, India, Japan, South Korea, and New Zealand—would then need to attempt to coordinate their trade and FDI regimes. India, which has only recently moved away from its former protectionist stance, would also need to attempt to coordinate deeper structural and regulatory reforms addressing both tariff issues and "behind-the-border" red-tape issues.

A RCEP would likely be based on existing ASEAN+1 FTAs with the "plus-six" economies—Australia, China, India, Japan, New Zealand, and South Korea—as well as future networks of bilateral and/or multilateral FTAs among these "plus" economies. Five ASEAN+1 FTAs have been implemented, but not all FTAs among the "plus" economies have been completed.

For example, several bilateral and/or multilateral FTAs are patchy, and important components—such as a trilateral FTA among China, Japan, and South Korea or three bilateral FTAs among these three economies—are still missing (Table 1). Such FTAs would facilitate, as important building blocks, the formation of RCEP. From this perspective the successful formation of RCEP requires not only

Several bilateral and/or multilateral FTAs are patchy, and important components are still missing

the completion of ASEAN+1 FTAs but also a series of agreements among the "plus" economies, particularly among China, Japan, and South Korea (See Kawai and Wignaraja 2008). In principle, ASEAN+6 economies could begin RCEP negotiations without all these building blocks in place as such agreements might be created as elements of the RCEP negotiations.

Table 1. Bilateral and Multilateral FTAs (Status by Economy)							
	ASEAN	**India**	**Japan**	**South Korea**	**China**	**Australia**	**New Zealand**
ASEAN	◎	◎	◎	◎	◎	◎	
India	◎	–	◎	◎	△	△	△
Japan	◎	◎	–	○	△	○	×
South Korea	◎	◎	○	–	○	○	○
China	◎	△	△	○	–	○	◎
Australia	◎	△	○	○	○	–	◎
New Zealand		△	×	○	◎	◎	–

Source: ADB ARIC FTA database (www.aric.adb.org); data as of March 2012.

Notes: 1) ◎ = FTA in place or FTA negotiation signed

○ = official negotiations under way

△ = feasibility study of FTA under way

✕ = no official move taken.

2) Although Japan and South Korea launched an official negotiation in December 2003, it was suspended in November 2004 because of continuing significant differences. A new official feasibility study on a China-Japan-South Korea FTA was introduced in May 2010. An official consultation between Japan and South Korea is expected to be held seeking possible resumption of bilateral FTA negotiations. Late in 2013, China, Japan, and South Korea agreed to begin trilateral negotiations.

However, given that bilateral negotiations between China and Japan will likely take significant time, it might be preferable to conclude such laborious discussions before beginning official negotiations for RCEP.

Similarly, to begin the official negotiation for RCEP, it would be preferable first for India to conclude negotiations with Australia, China, and New Zealand.

If all such noted preliminary steps were to be successfully achieved, RCEP negotiations could lead to the formation of a single, larger Asian FTA through consolidation and harmonization of existing FTAs. While rationales differed for supporting either EAFTA or CEPEA, both proposals shared many similar elements.

An argument for supporting EAFTA was that Asia's production network was largely developed among the ASEAN+3 economies so harmonizing ROO among these economies would produce immediate benefits.

India, however, was perceived as being slow to liberalize trade policies so it might take more time to initially produce a region-wide FTA including India. Once EAFTA negotiations were well advanced there was reason to believe collective pressure would be more effective in encouraging India to further open its economy.

Alternatively, an argument for supporting CEPEA was that Asia's production network had already developed beyond the ASEAN+3 economies and already encompassed both Australia and India. Additionally, the economic benefits from FTA consolidation would be greater with CEPEA than with EAFTA.

The official study group considering EAFTA and/or CEPEA solutions agreed that the ASEAN+3 economies should focus on trade and investment liberalization as their first priority, trade and investment facilitation as their second priority, and technical cooperation as their third priority while the ASEAN+6 economies should focus on technical cooperation as their first priority, trade and investment liberalization as their second priority, and trade and investment facilitation as their third priority.

The study group's differentiation of priorities between EAFTA and CEPEA negotiations suggested that EAFTA was a likely first step to be followed by CEPEA. This sequenced approach was considered particularly realistic if India delayed liberalizing their behind-the-border regulations and investment and trade policies. Even though the ASEAN+6 countries agreed that they would negotiate on a Regional Comprehensive Economic Partnership(RCEP), putting priorities on the wider CEPEA, the actual process might proceed faster among the ASEAN+3 countries, Australia, and New Zealand than among the full ASEAN+6 countries.

A China-Japan-South Korea FTA

One of the most important preconditions for a RCEP would be the creation of a China-Japan-South Korea FTA either as a trilateral FTA among these economies or as three bilateral FTAs between pairs of these economies. There are, however, significant differences in enthusiasm for FTAs among these three economies. Japan and South Korea launched official EPA negotiations in December 2003 but suspended these negotiations in November 2004 because of significant continuing differences. In May 2012 negotiations began on a China–South Korea FTA and discussions on a China-Japan-South Korea FTA. The decision to begin these negotiations was encouraged, in part, by the advent of the TPP strongly supported by the United States. In November 2012, China, Japan, and South Korea indeed agreed to begin official negotiations.

Japan is concerned with the rising competitiveness of China's agricultural and manufacturing sectors. Japan wishes to treat China as a non-market economy to allow Japan's use of safeguard measures protecting against a rapid increase of Chinese exports into Japanese markets. China, however, insists upon being recognized as a market economy. Japan also argues that China has yet to demonstrate significant progress in implementing such WTO entry commitments as equitable treatment of Japanese enterprises in China, transparency of enterprise regulations and rules, and protection of intellectual property rights. Food-safety issues in China are also of concern to Japan.

Japan has insisted that an investment treaty be a first condition before beginning broader EPA negotiations. China, Japan, and South Korea have, in fact, been negotiating a trilateral investment treaty since March 2007 and are now reportedly close to reaching final agreement.

South Korea was also concerned about China's agricultural competitiveness,[26] South Korea's s excessive dependence on the Chinese market, and South Korea's lack of an overall policy on investment and trade with China. However, given the increasing momentum of TPP discussions and Japan's stated intension to join these TPP negotiations, China aggressively approached South Korea to convince it to begin bilateral FTA negotiations with China, and South Korea agreed.

Although Japan and South Korea are also interested in concluding an EPA with each other, each economy has concerns. Japan's primary concern regarding a Japan–South Korea EPA is the competitiveness of South Korea's agricultural and fishery sectors. In contrast, South Korea's primary concerns regarding Japan's competitiveness are manufactured products (intermediate inputs), large tariff concessions required from South Korea to address existing high most-favored-nation tariffs, and the risk of a greater South Korean bilateral trade deficit with Japan.

A major challenge for a China-Japan-South Korea FTA is whether Japan is willing to begin serious EPA negotiations with China and South Korea despite the concerns noted above. If Japan is forthcoming and the three economies can negotiate mutually agreeable FTAs they could provide a strong foundation for a possible RCEP. This would require substantial political commitments from the governments of all three economies.

> *Negotiations would require substantial political commitments from the governments of all three economies*

TPP

The United States has advocated strengthening economic ties among APEC members through the formation of an APEC-wide free trade area (i.e., FTAAP). FTAAP would increase two-way trade of partner economies in a significant manner. It could also serve as a useful step in reviving the currently stalled Doha Round trade talks or offer an alternative "Plan B" solution should the Doha Round trade talks fail (Bergsten 2007, Hufbauer and Schott 2009). Creation of FTAAP would likely take many years and assuredly involve multiple studies, evaluations, and negotiations among all 21 member economies. Given the large number of APEC members, a smaller group might more successfully initiate the process.

A recently emerging smaller FTA, the TPP, is attracting a growing number of economies sympathetic to its goal of high-standard liberalization (Markheim 2008). TPP started as the Pacific Four (P4) Agreement, a multilateral FTA among Brunei Darussalam, Chile, New Zealand, and Singapore that came into force May 2006.[27] The agreement eliminated 90 percent of all tariffs among member economies upon entry into force and will completely eliminate all trade tariffs by 2015.

In September 2008 the United States announced its intent to begin comprehensive negotiations with the P4 economies to join the agreement. Negotiations to expand P4 membership began in March 2010 with Australia, Peru, the United States, and Vietnam. Malaysia joined the talks in November 2010. More recently, Canada, Japan, Mexico, Philippines, Taipei, China, and Thailand have expressed interest in joining the talks. Canada and Mexico are expected to join the negotiations in 2013.

TPP is often viewed as a key element in a strategic United States pivot to Asia. Participation in TPP is projected to add billions to the US economy and solidify US military and political links with the Asia Pacific economies for future decades (Gordon 2012). Given its substantial potential benefits, TPP would appear to have a better chance of overcoming US domestic opposition (from trade unions and the US automotive industry) to trade liberalization than would the Doha Round trade talks or new bilateral FTAs.

The goal of an expanded TPP would be to achieve a comprehensive twenty-first-century FTA covering not only tariff reductions and services-trade liberalization but also a large number of WTO-plus issues such as competition, environmental and labor standards, intellectual property, investment, public procurement, sanitary and phytosanitary measures, and technical barriers to trade.

Regarding market access, in principle all tariffs are eliminated. Non-tariff barriers to trade will be substantially reduced and behind-the-border regulatory reforms would be pursued to guarantee domestic markets are open and transparent. TPP's broad framework was unveiled at the APEC summit in Hawai'i in November 2011.

TPP has the potential to include many other economies under the agreement's accession clause. Thus, TPP could help expand and strengthen economic and strategic ties among select APEC members and could provide the foundation for a wider FTAAP.

FTAAP

APEC remains important for both Asia and the United States because it is the only multilateral economic forum that bridges the two entities. The United States provides the most open market for Asian products as well as a security umbrella for key Asian economies. The United States has advocated forming an APEC-wide free trade area (FTAAP) and promoted this cause in APEC forums.

The 2010 APEC Leaders' Summit in Yokohama ended with a promise of further steps towards forming an APEC-wide free trade area. That summit also suggested that such a comprehensive FTAAP should be pursued by building on ongoing regional initiatives—notably ASEAN+3, ASEAN+6, East Asia Summit, and TPP.

The United States has also pursued bilateral FTAs with some Asian economies and has concluded bilateral FTAs with such economies as Australia, Singapore, and South Korea. However, despite serious attempts, the United States has not been able to reach agreements with other economies such as Malaysia or Thailand. Questions remain as to whether the United States is able to agree to an FTA with the whole of Asia—one that includes China—given the current US domestic political environment.

There are presently two alternative paths under consideration for creating FTAAP: using an expanded TPP or (as the second alternative) using RCEP. This study identified a number of impediments to pursuing either TPP or the ASEAN-centric alternative.

TPP faces the following issues: while APEC is a voluntary, non-binding organization, forming FTAs requires binding commitments to trade and investment liberalization from the participating economies. Unless the mandate of APEC were to change, this would indicate that an expanded TPP would need to be pursued outside of the existing formal APEC process.[28] Also the TPP alternative would reduce the importance of ASEAN centrality to Asian integration, given that not all ASEAN economies are APEC members. Currently, Brunei Darussalam, Malaysia, Singapore, and Vietnam are the ASEAN members actively involved in negotiating TPP. It appears unlikely that all other economies participating in both ASEAN and APEC—particularly Indonesia—would be able to join TPP within a reasonable time as TPP aims for high-standard and comprehensive liberalization measures. The extent of this problem would, of course, depend on the conclusions of TPP11, i.e., the eleven negotiating countries including Canada and Mexico as new members. Further, any TPP, while strongly transregional, would likely exclude China—the most dynamic economy in the region—and thus will fail to generate a fully inclusive FTAAP. Lastly, India is not an APEC member and would, therefore, require significant additional time to participate in any TPP.[29]

The ASEAN-centric alternative of forming RCEP also faces significant issues: RCEP is unlikely to adopt high-standard and comprehensive liberalization measures because participants include large developing economies—such as China, India, and Indonesia—not yet ready to accept significant investment and trade liberalization and open transparent rules and regulations. Also, by excluding the United States—still the most important economy in the Asia Pacific region from both economic and security perspectives—RCEP cannot become a full-fledged regional agreement directly leading to the formation of FTAAP.

These issues suggest that both alternatives—TPP and RCEP—must, at some point, converge to form an effective FTAAP. If the United States were to successfully conclude an FTA with ASEAN as an ASEAN+1 partner,[30] the convergence process could well be substantially accelerated. But more importantly, convergence requires China to be ready to accept high-level liberalization of, and transparent rules over, trade and investment. It will also require the United States to accept China as a responsible trade and investment partner.

> *These issues suggest that TPP and RCEP must converge to form an effective FTAAP*

Links with Europe

In recent years economic ties between Asia and the EU have rapidly expanded. Two-way trade has doubled over the last five years and the EU economies are among the most significant foreign investors in Asia. When compared, however, to APEC's efforts in investment and trade facilitation and liberalization, the Asia-Europe Meeting has been much less active addressing transregional investment and trade liberalization. Only since 2007 has the EU initiated negotiations on trade agreements with Asia. The EU and South Korea implemented the EU's first Asian FTA in July 2011. The EU has also been negotiating FTAs with ASEAN and India and is about to launch EPA negotiations with Japan.

The South Korea–EU FTA is one of the most comprehensive and high-level agreements ever negotiated with an Asian economy, going much further than WTO commitments and eliminating 97 percent of all tariff barriers within three years. Initially the EU attempted to generate a single FTA with ASEAN but later changed its strategy to negotiating separate FTAs with individual ASEAN members. This shift in approach reflected the economic diversity and heterogeneity among ASEAN economies.

EU-India FTA negotiations are slowing in the face of a number of challenges: the EU wants India to liberalize investment, public procurement, and services-trade policies while India wants the EU to relax its stringent food-safety criteria and immigration policy with regard to Indian professionals.

After lengthy consultations regarding Japan's non-tariff barriers to investment and trade, the EU has agreed to begin official FTA negotiation with Japan.

Though connecting Asia with the EU is a relatively recent effort, should the EU decide to negotiate an FTA with China—building on its FTAs with South Korea and, possibly, ASEAN economies, India, and Japan—a solid foundation for FTAs linking Asia with Europe could be developed.

Unfortunately, given the current Eurozone economic crisis, this process may take considerable time. The EU presently appears preoccupied with resolving multiple sovereign-debt and banking-sector crises and shoring up the euro rather than focusing on external trade policies. However, EU will gain substantially by connecting it with the growing Asian region in the midst of uncertain global economic conditions.

A Likely Scenario: Sequencing of FTA Consolidation

FTA consolidation in Asia may proceed along the lines of an ASEAN-centric RCEP and TPP. The following consolidation sequence might be a likely scenario:

- the acceleration of an ASEAN Economic Community (AEC) to be created by 2015;
- the creation of a China-Japan-South Korea FTA either directly through a China-Japan-South Korea trilateral agreement or through bilateral agreements among the three economies;
- the formation of RCEP among the ASEAN+6 economies through mechanisms connecting the existing ASEAN+1 FTAs, a new China-Japan-South Korea FTA, and other bilateral FTAs

among the "plus six"countries by allowing the combining, harmonizing, and simplifying of ROO;[31]

- the formation of TPP and expansion of its membership within the Asia-Pacific region; and
- the connection of RCEP with TPP to form FTAAP—and with the EU to form FTAAE.

The dynamics of this "likely scenario" would evolve over time with each step creating incentives and momentum for the next. The completion of an AEC is vital to FTA consolidation in Asia. This would strengthen the ability of ASEAN to serve as the region's integration hub. Once AEC is in place, further promoting ASEAN economic integration, ASEAN would become a more coherent entity. Building on this strength, ASEAN FTAs would be expected to improve substantially in quality.

Moving from ASEAN FTAs to a full customs union would likely be difficult as it would require all members agreeing to a common external tariff where members presently use quite different tariffs (Appendix Table 1). Some economies (e.g., Singapore) could be required to raise import tariffs while others (e.g., Cambodia and Thailand) could be required to lower such barriers. Nonetheless, a full customs union is a desired direction for ASEAN after the completion of an AEC.

The creation of a China-Japan-South Korea FTA is needed for the formation of RCEP because it would be otherwise impossible to formally integrate the ASEAN+3 economies. A political decision by China and Japan (and South Korea) to form a bilateral (or trilateral) FTA would be the required cornerstone agreement.

ASEAN may play a key role in encouraging these two leading economies (and South Korea) to agree to a Northeast Asian FTA. Once a China-Japan-South Korea FTA (or at least a bilateral FTA/ EPA between China and Japan) is formed it could be connected with ASEAN+1 FTAs through various mechanisms allowing the combining, harmonizing, and simplifying of ROO.

The formation of RCEP would also require, among other factors, a bilateral FTA between China and India.

It would be easier to connect Asia with the United States and the EU

Separate from the RCEP and TPP sequencing discussed above, it would be easier to eventually connect the whole of Asia with the United States (possibly through FTAAP) and with the EU (possibly through FTAAE) once the United States and the EU have concluded FTAs with several key Asian economies.

Such sequenced approaches are important and would potentially accelerate the process of Asia's intraregional economic integration as well as its transregional economic integration with Europe and North America.

Conclusion

This study has addressed challenges, prospects, and trends associated with the spread of Asian FTAs. It has offered new evidence detailing Asian FTA use through the analysis of such agreements, CGE results, and enterprise-level surveys as well as considered political-economy issues and various competing proposals.

The evidence demonstrates a shift in Asian trade policy occurring since 2000. With 71 concluded agreements, FTAs are assuming ever greater importance as tools of Asian commercial policy. Singapore and the region's three largest economies are identified as key to the growing Asian FTA activity while ASEAN, as an organization, is emerging as an integration hub for such efforts. Asian FTAs have maintained strong cross-regional orientations, their trade coverage has increased, and broader issues than simply trade liberalization—including competition, intellectual property, investment, labor standards, mobility, and public procurement—have been addressed.

Successful conclusion of comprehensive Doha Round trade talks would be an invaluable contribution to global, including Asian, prosperity (for recent restatements of this case see Hoekman, Martin, and Mattoo 2009; Bhagwati and Sutherland 2011). However the outcome of the currently stalled global trade talks remains uncertain and the eventual result may be significantly limited negotiations.

With the large number of FTAs concluded, under negotiation, or proposed, Asian FTAs are here to stay. Maximizing the benefits of these Asian FTAs while minimizing their costs would be highly pragmatic. Given the observations of this study, key elements of pragmatic responses to Asian FTAs might include:

- increasing the use of FTAs through improved awareness and strengthened institutional support, particularly for SMEs, and creating a regional database on FTA use;
- addressing the Asian noodle bowl through greater rationalization of ROO and upgrading ROO administration to best-practice levels;
- encouraging greater coverage of agricultural products in Asian FTAs and supporting gradual increases in liberalizing agricultural-trade policies;
- facilitating gradual increases in liberalizing services-trade policies through emphasis on key GATS sectors;
- including WTO-plus provisions—particularly the four Singapore issues—in all future Asian FTAs; and
- facilitating the creation of a region-wide agreement in East Asia—particularly RCEP—with appropriate sub-sequencing and support for development gaps among members.

While the economic case for a region-wide agreement such as RCEP is clearly supported by CGE analysis, political-economy considerations will continue to heavily influence any outcome. With key ASEAN+1 FTAs currently in place, a realistic consolidation sequence of discrete steps within Asia would include strengthening ASEAN economic integration, generating a China-Japan-South Korea FTA, and combining ASEAN+1 FTAs with a China-Japan-South Korea FTA. These steps would be followed by forging RCEP and then connecting Asia with Europe and North America.

To connect Asia with Europe, a series of bilateral FTAs with the EU would be useful. To connect Asia with North America, TPP and a series of bilateral FTAs with the United States would be similarly useful.

As geopolitics rather than economics will likely determine the actual steps, unknown events may overwhelm this projected sequence. Actual developments may well not be as orderly, neat, or rational as those described above. The reality could easily become substantially more complex.

A region-wide agreement could ultimately turn out to be a series of linked agreements with varying members and issues. This study suggests that a bottom-up approach to global investment and trade integration, complementing the existing top-down process, be adopted.

Appendix Tables

Appendix Table 1. Per-capita Income and Trade Policy in Asia

	Per-capita Income, PPP (current US$)		Share of World GDP, PPP (by Percent)		Simple Mean, MFN Tariff Rate (by Percent)		Concluded FTAs (by No. of FTAs)		Trade Coverage of FTAs (by Percent of Total Trade)	
	2000	2011	2000	2011	2000	2010	2010	2012	2000	2010
Northeast Asia										
China	2,379	8,382	7.13	14.32	17.0	9.7	1	12	8.2	27.0
Hong Kong	26,180	49,137	0.42	0.45	0.0	0.0	0	3	0.0	45.5
Japan	25,669	34,740	7.70	5.63	4.3	3.1	0	13	0.0	11.3
South Korea	16,503	31,714	1.83	1.97	12.7	12.4	1	9	10.4	42.4
Taiwan	20,290	37,720	1.07	1.11	9.5	6.1	0	5	0.0	15.0
ASEAN										
Brunei Darussalam	43,320	49,384	0.03	0.03	3.8	2.5	1	8	33.9	94.4
Cambodia	908	2,216	0.03	0.04	16.4	14.2	1	6	24.8	62.1
Indonesia	2,429	4,666	1.19	1.43	8.4	6.7	1	9	18.2	66.1
Lao PDR	1,180	2,659	0.02	0.02	9.5	9.7	3	8	65.0	84.7
Malaysia	9,174	15,568	0.51	0.57	8.3	8.6	1	12	25.4	51.2
Myanmar	459	1,325	0.05	0.11	5.5	5.6	1	6	35.8	90.2
Philippines	2,442	4,073	0.44	0.50	7.6	6.3	1	7	15.6	60.5
Singapore	32,262	59,711	0.32	0.40	0.0	0.0	1	20	26.3	70.8
Thailand	5,007	9,396	0.73	0.76	18.4	10.4	2	12	18.1	56.6
Vietnam	1,424	3,359	0.26	0.38	16.5	9.8	1	8	23.5	57.4

Appendix Table 1. Per-capita Income and Trade Policy in Asia (continued)

India	1,534	3,694	3.72	5.65	34.6	14.0	1	13	6.1	22.6
Memorandum items										
US	35,252	48,387	23.53	19.13	4.1	3.8	1	20	-	25.9
EU-27	21,885	32,642	24.94	20.25	5.7	4.2	15	31	-	34.2

Sources: World Bank, World Development Indicators; ADB, Asia Regional Integration Center; IMF, Direction of Trade Statistics; IMF, World Economic Outlook Database; US Trade Representative (http://www.ustr.gov); EU Trade (http://ec.europa.eu)

Appendix Table 2. Use of FTAs in Thailand and Vietnam, 2011[a]		
FTA	**Thailand**	**Vietnam**
Total FTA Use	61%	31%
By FTA		
ASEAN (AFTA)	52%	20%
Australia (AANZFTA)	27%	16%[b]
Australia (TAFTA)	91%	
China (ACFTA)	85%	23%
India (AIFTA)	28%	7%
India (TIFTA)	75%	
Japan (AJCEP)	4%	31%
Japan (JTEPA)	72%	
New Zealand (AANZFTA)	18%	16%[b]
South Korea (AKFTA)	59%	91%

Sources: Udomwichaiwat (2012) for Thailand and Tran (2012) for Vietnam

Notes: a) official data from certificate of origin

b) combined use rate for Australia and New Zealand. Breakdown not provided

Appendix Table 3. Coverage of Selected FTAs in Asia

Provisions — A. GOODS	Tariff Elimination	ROO	Trade Remedies—Anti Dumping	Trade Remedies—Subsidies and Countervailing	Trade Remedies—Bilateral Safeguards	Agriculture	Apparel and Textiles	Quarantine and SPS Measures	Other Non-tariff Measures
SINGAPORE									
Transpacific Strategic EPA (2006)	■	■	■	■	■	■	□	■	■
US-Singapore FTA (2004)	■	■	□	□	■	■	□	■	■
EFTA-Singapore FTA (2003)	■	■	■	■	■	■	■	□	■
New Zealand–Singapore CEP (2001)	■	■	■	■	■	■	■	■	□
SOUTH KOREA									
South Korea–US FTA (2012)	■	■	■	■	■	■	■	■	■
South Korea–EU FTA (2011)	■	■	■	■	■	■	■	■	■
South Korea–Singapore FTA (2006)	■	■	■	■	■	■	■	■	□
South Korea–Chile FTA (2004)	■	■	■	□	■	■	■	■	■
ASEAN–South Korea CECA (2007)	■	■	■	■	■	□	■	■	■
JAPAN									
India-Japan EPA (2011)	■	■	■	■	■	■	□	■	■
ASEAN-Japan CEPA (2008)	■	■	■	■	■	■	■	■	■
Japan-Philippines EPA (2008)	■	■	□	□	■	■	■	■	□
Japan-Chile FTA (2007)	■	■	■	■	■	■	■	■	■
Japan-Mexico EPA (2005)	■	■	■	■	■	■	■	■	■
Japan-Singapore EPA (2002)	■	■	□	□	■	■	□	■	■
INDIA									
India–South Korea FTA (2010)	■	■	■	■	■	■	□	■	■
South Asian FTA (2006)	■	■	■	□	■	■	■	■	■
India-Mercosur FTA (2004)	■	■	■	■	■	■	■	■	■
India–Sri Lanka FTA (2000)	■	■	■	■	■	□	■	■	■
CHINA									
China-Taiwan FTA (2010)	■	■	□	■	■	■	■	■	■
China–New Zealand FTA (2008)	■	■	■	■	■	■	■	■	■
China-Pakistan FTA (2007)	■	■	■	■	■	■	■	■	■
China-Chile FTA (2006)	■	■	■	■	■	□	■	■	■
ASEAN-China CECA (2005)	■	■	■	■	■	■	■	■	■
ASEAN FTA (1992)	■	■	□	□	■	■	□	□	□

Appendix Table 3. Coverage of Selected FTAs in Asia (continued)

	Technical Barriers to Trade	Standards and Conformance, MRAs	Customs Administration and Procedures			Telecommunications	Financial Services	Professional Services	Labor Mobility/Entry of Business Persons	
SINGAPORE						**B. SERVICES**				
Transpacific Strategic EPA (2006)	■	■	■			■	■	■	■	
US-Singapore FTA (2004)	■	■	■			■	■		■	
EFTA-Singapore FTA (2003)	■	■				■	■	■		
New Zealand–Singapore CEP (2001)	■	■	■			■				
SOUTH KOREA										
South Korea–US FTA (2012)	■	■	■			■	■	■	■	
South Korea–EU FTA (2011)	■	■				■	■	■	■	
South Korea–Singapore FTA (2006)	■	■	■			■	■	■	■	
South Korea–Chile FTA (2004)	■	■	■			■		■	■	
ASEAN–South Korea CECA (2007)	■					■	■	■	■	
JAPAN										
India-Japan EPA (2011)	■						■	■	■	
ASEAN-Japan CEPA (2008)	■	■	■							
Japan-Philippines EPA (2008)	■		■			■	■	■	■	
Japan-Chile FTA (2007)	■					■	■	■	■	
Japan-Mexico EPA (2005)		■	■			■	■	■	■	
Japan-Singapore EPA (2002)	■		■			■	■	■	■	
INDIA										
India–South Korea FTA (2010)	■	■	■			■	■	■	■	
South Asian FTA (2006)		■	■							
India-Mercosur FTA (2004)	■	■								
India–Sri Lanka FTA (2000)		■								
CHINA										
China-Taiwan FTA (2010)	■					■	■	■	■	
China–New Zealand FTA (2008)	■	■				■	■	■	■	
China-Pakistan FTA (2007)	■	■								
China-Chile FTA (2006)	■									
ASEAN-China CECA (2005)	■					■	■	■		
ASEAN FTA (1992)	■	■	■							

Appendix Table 3. Coverage of Selected FTAs in Asia (continued)

C. SINGAPORE ISSUES

- Intellectual Property
- Investment
- Public Procurement
- Competition

D. COOPERATION ENHANCEMENT

- Intellectual Property
- ICT and e-Commerce
- Labor Standards/Movement of Natural Persons
- Environment
- ECOTECH
- Capacity Building
- Information Exchange
- Energy
- Communications and Transport
- Construction
- SMEs
- Investment and Trade Promotion
- State Trading Enterprises

Appendix Table 3. Coverage of Selected FTAs in Asia (continued)

Country	FTA	Education	Transparency	Dispute Settlement	Percent of Goods and Services Provisions Covered (A+B)	Percent of WTO-plus Provisions Covered (C+D)
CHINA	ASEAN FTA (1992)				44	5
CHINA	ASEAN-China CECA (2005)				81	5
CHINA	China-Chile FTA (2006)				56	37
CHINA	China-Pakistan FTA (2007)				63	11
CHINA	China–New Zealand FTA (2008)				94	42
CHINA	China-Taiwan FTA (2010)				38	20
INDIA	India–Sri Lanka FTA (2000)				31	5
INDIA	India-Mercosur FTA (2004)				63	5
INDIA	South Asian FTA (2006)				50	5
INDIA	India–South Korea FTA (2010)				94	90
JAPAN	Japan-Singapore EPA (2002)				75	53
JAPAN	Japan-Mexico EPA (2005)				56	47
JAPAN	Japan-Chile FTA (2007)				88	32
JAPAN	Japan-Philippines EPA (2008)				69	58
JAPAN	ASEAN-Japan CEPA (2008)				69	58
JAPAN	India-Japan EPA (2011)				69	85
SOUTH KOREA	ASEAN–South Korea CECA (2007)				56	5
SOUTH KOREA	South Korea–Chile FTA (2004)				75	26
SOUTH KOREA	South Korea–Singapore FTA (2006)				81	63
SOUTH KOREA	South Korea–EU FTA (2011)				88	85
SOUTH KOREA	South Korea–US FTA (2012)				100	58
SINGAPORE	New Zealand–Singapore CEP (2001)				63	37
SINGAPORE	EFTA-Singapore FTA (2003)				81	26
SINGAPORE	US-Singapore FTA (2004)				56	47
SINGAPORE	Transpacific Strategic EPA (2006)				75	47

Source: FTA legal texts available at ADB's Asia Regional Integration Center (ARIC) FTA Database (www.aric.adb.org), data as of 3 April 2012.

Notes: ADB = Asian Development Bank; ASEAN = Association of Southeast Asian Nations; CECA = Comprehensive Economic Cooperation Agreement; CEP = comprehensive economic partnership; CEPA = comprehensive economic partnership agreement; ECOTECH = economic and technical cooperation; EFTA = European Free Trade Area; EPA = economic partnership agreement; FTA = free trade agreement; ICT = information and communications technology; Mercosur = Common Market of the South; MRA = mutual recognition agreement; ROO = rules of origin; SME = small- and medium-sized enterprise; SPS = sanitary and phytosanitary standards; US = United States; WTO = World Trade Organization.

Appendix Table 4. CEPEA Scenario—Changes in Output Across Broad Sectors Compared to Projected 2017 Baseline, by Percent

	Thailand	Vietnam	South Korea	Malaysia	Singapore	Philippines	Indonesia
AGRICULTURE & FOOD	-1.2	-6.3	10.5	-1.2	64.8	0.3	-0.2
OTHER PRIMARY	0.5	0.4	0.7	0.6	0.3	0.5	0.4
MANUFACTURES	9.3	49.9	5.5	5.7	1.5	10.6	2.4
textiles & clothing	3.2	63.1	26.3	2.6	-14.3	12.4	1.9
metals	22.0	12.1	11.8	24.4	16.7	-2.3	-1.2
electrical machinery	25.8	11.5	2.4	-0.4	1.2	2.0	7.1
motor vehicles	10.6	-28.9	2.5	-3.3	-28.4	-18.2	-6.5
SERVICES	13.3	16.0	5.8	4.7	4.5	4.0	2.9

	India	Japan	China	Cambodia	Other ASEAN	Hong Kong	Taiwan
AGRICULTURE & FOOD	0.5	-2.1	-0.4	-4.1	0.9	0.2	0.7
OTHER PRIMARY	0.3	1.3	0.2	0.1	0.3	0.4	1.9
MANUFACTURES	5.9	0.6	2.4	55.2	-2.9	-10.2	-2.4
clothing & textiles	-1.5	5.8	2.7	-2.1	-3.5	-13.1	-17.5
metals	15.6	6.5	-1.4	69.4	-8.0	-6.1	2.0
electrical machinery	1.8	-8.8	13.2	-17.4	5.5	-21.4	-4.5
motor vehicles	-2.1	0.5	-5.6	-7.7	-2.1	1.8	0.0
SERVICES	4.2	1.1	2.4	3.1	0.2	0.2	-1.6

Source: Estimates based on the CGE model used in Francois and Wignaraja (2008).

Note: CEPEA = Comprehensive Economic Partnership for East Asia.

Endnotes

1. See Freund and Ornelas (2010) and WTO (2011) for a review of theoretical and empirical literature on FTAs and Chia (2010) for the literature on Asian FTAs.

2. For the purposes of this paper, the term "Asia" is narrowly used to describe 16 economies in East Asia and India, while the term "developing Asia" excludes Japan. More specifically, "Asia" includes: the 10 ASEAN member economies (Brunei Darussalam; Cambodia; Indonesia; Lao People's Democratic Republic [Lao PDR]; Malaysia; Myanmar; Philippines; Singapore; Thailand; and Vietnam); the Asian newly industrialized economies other than Singapore (i.e., Hong Kong, South Korea, and Taiwan); China; India; and Japan.

3. Appendix Table 1 also shows that the majority of Asian economies have undertaken notable tariff cuts but double-digit average MFN tariffs were visible in some (e.g., Cambodia, India, South Korea, and Thailand) in 2010.

4. The members are Bangladesh, China, India, Lao PDR, Nepal, Philippines, South Korea, and Sri Lanka.

5. More complete explanations can be found in Kawai (2005), Dent (2006), Sally (2008), ADB (2008 and 2010), Chia (2010), and Zhang and Shen (2011).

6. Brunei Darussalam, Chile, India, Indonesia, Malaysia, Mexico, Philippines, Singapore, Switzerland, Thailand, and Vietnam.

7. On this point, see Fiorentino, Crawford, and Toqueboeuf (2009).

8. We are grateful for Richard Baldwin for this suggestion.

9. In Singapore's case, the high ratio reflects a proactive strategy of concluding a large number of bilateral and ASEAN FTAs. In Brunei Darussalam, Lao PDR, and Myanmar, this ratio may suggest high commodity dependence and market concentration in a limited export base.

10. Intra-EU trade is excluded from this figure.

11. Others suggest that the depiction of Asian FTAs as a complicated "noodle bowl" is misleading. It has been argued that Asian FTAs may be creating an order of a different sort by building the foundation for a stronger regional trading system (Petri 2008, Chia 2010).

12. Harmonized ROO means the same rules of origin are applied across multiple FTAs. Co-equal ROO means alternative ROO for the same product are available in an FTA and enterprises are free to choose between them. Accumulation of value content provisions allows the use of non-domestic inputs from a specific economy or group of economies (with such inputs taken as originating in the FTA partner economy claiming origin) as determining the products origin. See Kawai and Wignaraja (2011b).

13. The data exclude FTAs involving Indonesia-Pakistan and Chile-Vietnam for which texts were not available.

14. Rice (a key sensitive sector), however, was excluded from the South Korea–US FTA agreement.

15. Lao PDR excludes 5 items, Vietnam 7, Malaysia 16, Philippines 17, Indonesia 24, and Cambodia and Myanmar 36 each. In contrast, Brunei Darussalam and Singapore eliminated tariffs on all agricultural products.

16. Positive and negative list approaches facilitate the identification of products/services for inclusion in FTAs and the extent of their coverage. A negative list approach liberalizes all sectors/products (in a phased manner) unless otherwise specified. A positive list approach is the stipulation of a specific number of products/sectors for preferential treatment with details of the extent of liberalization given to each item.

17. Future research can extend Fink and Molinuevo's (2008) more detailed review of key architectural choices in East Asian FTAs with a services component (e.g., dispute settlement, movement of natural persons, scheduling commitments, and treatment of investments) to analyzing the 69 Asian FTAs.

18. Namely, cross-border trade in services (mode 1); consumption abroad (mode 2); commercial presence (mode 3); and temporary movement of natural persons (mode 4).

19. Six FTAs involved Singapore, which typically covers the five key services in its FTAs. A similar approach was followed in the Taiwan-Panama FTA, the Japan-Mexico FTA, and the Thailand-Australia FTA. The ASEAN Framework Agreement on Services (AFAS) was signed in 1995/6 and the protocol to amend AFAS was launched in 2003. Thereafter, several rounds of negotiations have aimed at deepening AFAS.

20. An early review of 11 Asian agreements concluded that "modern FTAs in Asia, some of which are the most sophisticated in the world, have tended to be more comprehensive in terms of coverage and of the building bloc rather than the stumbling bloc type, though there are some (minor) exceptions in terms of certain components" (Plummer 2007, 1795). The study suggested a set of best practices to guide future FTAs.

21. The members are Brunei Darussalam, Chile, New Zealand, and Singapore.

22. ECOTECH is the APEC schedule of programs designed to build capacity and skills in APEC member economies to enable them to participate more fully in the regional economy and the liberalization process. See http://www.apec.org for more information.

23. Our overall findings broadly echo those of Lee, Owen, and van der Mensbrugghe (2009), whose sophisticated CGE study incorporates tariff reduction, trade-cost reduction, and endogenously determined productivity levels. These authors also suggested that the CEPEA scenario yields larger gains (US$201 billion) than the EAFTA scenario (US$177 billion) and that participants will gain while losses to non-participants will be negligible. Petri, Plummer, and Zhai's (2011) CGE model includes possibilities for increasing varieties of goods and services and for shifting resources among enterprises with heterogeneous productivity within each sector. They report welfare gains for TPP of US$104 billion, US$303 billion for both EAFTA and TPP, and US$862 billion with FTAAP.

24. As Lee, Owen, and van der Mensbrugghe (2009) observed, a worthwhile but difficult extension of CGE models on region-wide Asian FTAs would be to endogenize FDI flows involving Asian economies. Consistent data on bilateral FDI flows in Asia are, however, lacking.

25. Although the initial negotiation members of a RCEP have not been made explicit, they are generally understood to be ASEAN+6 counties, including the 10 ASEAN member states plus Australia, China, India, Japan, New Zealand, and South Korea.

26. Interestingly, South Korean farmers do not seem overly threatened by the South Korea–US FTA but express concerns over agriculture with regard to a South Korea–China FTA.

27. The TPP, previously known as the Pacific Three Closer Economic Partnership (P3-CEP), among Chile, New Zealand, and Singapore, launched its first negotiations at the 2002 APEC Leaders' Summit. In April 2005, Brunei Darussalam joined, and the original agreement was signed by the four countries in June 2005. Then the trade bloc became known as the Pacific Four.

28. Changing APEC's mandate into a prospective FTA organization would, however, likely encounter strong opposition from China and many middle-income ASEAN economies.

29. TPP lacks clarity concerning the extent of expansion of its membership but there is a presumption that it is open to APEC members willing to accept the TPP-negotiated text and ready to undertake its ambitious liberalization goals.

30. The United States signed ASEAN's Treaty of Amity and Cooperation in July 2009. This was a significant political step in strengthening this bilateral relationship. This provides a strong foundation for the United States becoming a legitimate ASEAN+1 partner.

31. Australia and New Zealand may join this process if they complete FTAs with the "plus-three" economies. Doing so would make the grouping "ASEAN+5." Additionally, should India similarly complete FTAs individually with all the "plus" economies then India, as well, could participate in the process to form CEPEA, bypassing the necessity to create EAFTA.

Bibliography

ADB. 2008. *Emerging Asian Regionalism: A Partnership for Shared Prosperity.* Manila: Asian Development Bank.

————. 2010. *Institutions for Regional Integration: Toward an Asian Economic Community.* Manila: Asian Development Bank.

ADB, ADBI. 2012. "Malaysia FTA Survey" mimeograph. Tokyo: Asian Development Bank.

ADB, IDB, and ADBI. 2012. *Shaping the Future of the Asia and the Pacific–Latin America and the Caribbean Relationship.* Tokyo and Washington, DC: Asian Development Bank Institute and Inter-American Development Bank.

Athukorala, P. 2011. "Production Networks and Trade Patterns in East Asia: Regionalization or Globalization?" *Asian Economic Papers* 10 (1): 65–95.

Baldwin, R. 2006. "Multilateralizing Regionalism: Spaghetti Bowls as Building Blocks on the Path to Global Free Trade." *World Economy* 29 (11): 1451–1518.

Banda, O.G.D., and J. Whalley. 2005. *Beyond Goods and Services: Competition Policy, Investment, Mutual Recognition, Movement of Persons, and Broader Cooperation Provisions of Recent FTAs involving ASEAN Countries.* NBER Working Paper Series 11232 (March). Cambridge: National Bureau of Economic Research.

Bchir, M., and M. Fouquin. 2006. *Economic Integration in Asia: Bilateral Free Trade Agreements Versus Asian Single Market.* CEPII Discussion Papers 15 (October). Paris: Centre d'Etudes Prospectives et d'Informations Internationales.

Bergsten, C.F. 2007. "Toward a Free Trade Area of the Asia Pacific." *Policy Briefs in International Economics* PB07-02 (September). Washington, DC: Peter G. Peterson Institute for International Economics.

Bhagwati, J.N. 1995. *US Trade Policy: The Infatuation with FTAs.* Columbia University Discussion Paper Series 726. New York: Columbia University.

————. 2008. *Termites in the Trading System: How Preferential Agreements Undermine Free Trade.* Oxford: Oxford University Press.

Bhagwati, J.N. and P. Sutherland. 2011. *The Doha Round: Setting a Deadline, Defining a Final Deal.* High Level Experts Group Interim Report. www.number10.gov.uk/wp-content/uploads/doha-round-jan-2011.pdf

Cheong, I. and J. Cho. 2006. "Market Access in FTAs: Assessment Based on Rules of Origin and Agricultural Trade Liberalization." *RIETI Discussion Paper Series* 07-E-016. Tokyo: The Research Institute of Economy, Trade and Industry.

Chia, S.Y. 2010. *Regional Trade Policy Cooperation and Architecture in East Asia.* ADBI Working Paper Series 191 (September). Tokyo: Asian Development Bank Institute.

Chirathivat, S. 2008. *Thailand's Strategy Towards FTAs in the New Context of East Asian Economic Integration.* A paper prepared for ADB, ADBI, and ERIA Joint Conference on the Asian Noodle Bowl (July 17–18). Tokyo: Asian Development Bank Institute.

Dent, C. 2006. *New Free Trade Agreements in the Asia-Pacific.* Basingstoke (UK): Palgrave Macmillan.

Drysdale, P. and S. Armstrong. 2010. "International and Regional Cooperation: Asia's Role and Responsibilities." *Asian Economic Policy Review* 5 (2): 157–73.

Ernst, D. 2004. *Late Innovation Strategies in Asian Electronics Industries: A Conceptual Framework and Illustrative Evidence.* East West Center Working Papers 66 (March).

Estevadeordal, A., and K. Suominen. 2006. "Mapping and Measuring Rules of Origin around the World." In *The Origin of Goods: Rules of Origin in Regional Trade Agreements*, edited by O. Cadot, A. Estevadeordal, A. Suwa-Eisenmann, and T. Verdier. Oxford: Oxford University Press.

Feridhanusetyawan, T. 2005. *Preferential Trade Agreements in the Asia-Pacific Region.* IMF Working Paper WP/05/149 (July). Washington, DC: International Monetary Fund.

Findlay, C., R. Ochiai and P. Dee. 2009. "Integrating Services Markets" in *Pan-Asian Integration: Linking East and South Asia*, edited by J. Francois, P. Rana and G.Wignaraja. Basingstoke (UK): Palgrave Macmillan.

Fink, C. and M. Molinuevo. 2008. "East Asian Free Trade Agreements in Services: Key Architectural Elements." *Journal of International Economic Law* 11 (2): 263–311.

Fiorentino, R.V., J. Crawford, and C. Toqueboeuf. 2009. "The Landscape of Regional Trade Agreements and WTO Surveillance." In *Multilateralizing Regionalism: Challenges for the Global Trading System*, edited by R. Baldwin and P. Low. Cambridge: Cambridge University Press.

Freund, C., and Ornelas, E. 2010. *Regional Trade Agreements.* World Bank Policy Research Working Papers 5314. Washington, DC: World Bank.

Francois, J.F., and G. Wignaraja. 2008. "Economic Implications of Asian Integration." *Global Economy Journal* 6 (3): 1–46.

Gilbert, J., R. Scollay, and B. Bora. 2004. "New Regional Trading Developments in the Asia-Pacific Region." In *Global Change and East Asian Policy Initiatives*, edited by S. Yusuf, M.A. Altaf, and N. Nabeshima. Washington, DC: World Bank.

Gordon, B.K. 2012. "Trading Up in Asia: Why the United States Needs the Trans-Pacific Partnership," *Foreign Affairs* (July/August).

Hiratsuka, D. 2011. *Production Networks in the Asia-Pacific Region: Facts and Policy Implications.* IDE-JETRO Discussion Paper 315. Tokyo: Institute of Developing Economies.

Hobday, M. 1995. *Innovation in East Asia: The Challenge to Japan.* Cheltenham (UK): Edward Elgar.

Hoekman, B., W. Martin, and A. Mattoo. 2009. *Conclude Doha: It Matters.* World Bank Policy Research Working Papers 5135. Washington, DC: World Bank.

Hoekman, B. and A. Mattoo. 2011. *Services Trade Liberalization and Regulatory Reform: Re-invigorating International Cooperation.* World Bank Policy Research Working Papers 5517. Washington, DC: World Bank.

Hufbauer, G., and J. Schott. 2009. "Fitting Asia-Pacific Agreements into the WTO System." In *Multilateralizing Regionalism: Challenges for the Global Trading System,* edited by R. Baldwin and P. Low. Cambridge: Cambridge University Press.

Kawai, M. 2005. "East Asian Economic Regionalism: Progress and Challenges." *Journal of Asian Economics* 16 (1, September): 29–55.

Kawai, M., and G. Wignaraja. 2008. "EAFTA or CEPEA? Which Way Forward?" *ASEAN Economic Bulletin* 25 (2): 113–39.

———. 2009a. "Multilateralizing Regional Trading Arrangements in Asia." In *Multilateralizing Regionalism: Challenges for the Global Trading System,* edited by R. Baldwin and P. Low. Cambridge: Cambridge University Press.

———. 2009b. *The Asian Noodle Bowl: Is It Serious for Business?* ADBI Working Paper Series 136 (April). Tokyo: Asian Development Bank Institute.

———. 2011a. "Asian FTAs: Trends, Prospects and Challenges," *Journal of Asian Economics* 22: 1–22.

———. 2011b. *Asia's Free Trade Agreements: How Is Business Responding?* Cheltenham (UK): Edward Elgar.

Kawai, M., and F. Zhai. 2010. "Asia's Post-Global Financial Crisis Adjustment: A Model-Based Dynamic Scenario Analysis." *Asian Development Review* 27 (2): 122–51.

Kawai, M., and S. Urata. 2012. "Japan's Commercial Policy." In *The Oxford Handbook of International Commercial Policy,* edited by M. Kreinin and M. Plummer. Oxford: Oxford University Press.

Kimura, F. 2006. "International Production and Distribution Networks in East Asia: Eighteen Facts, Mechanics, and Policy Implications." *Asian Economic Policy Review* 1 (2): 326–44.

Koh, T. and C.L. Lin, eds. 2004. *The United States–Singapore Free Trade Agreement: Highlights and Insights.* Singapore: Institute of Policy Studies and World Scientific Publishing Co. Ltd.

Kunimoto, R., and G. Sawchuk. 2005. *NAFTA Rules of Origin.* Policy Research Initiative Discussion Paper (June). Ottawa: Policy Research Initiative.

Lall, S. 1992. "Technological Capabilities and Industrialization." *World Development* 20 (2): 165–86.

———. 2000. "The Technology Structure and Performance of Developing Country Manufactured Exports." *Oxford Development Studies* 28:337–69.

Lee, H., R.F. Owen, and D. van der Mensbrugghe. 2009. "Regional Integration in Asia and Its Effects on the EU and North America." *Journal of Asian Economics* 20 (3): 240–54.

Lim, C.K., D.K. Elms, and P. Low, eds. 2012. *The Trans-Pacific Partnership: A Quest for a Twenty-first Century Trade Agreement.* Cambridge: Cambridge University Press.

Lin, J.F. 2012. *The Quest for Prosperity: How Developing Economies Can Take Off.* Princeton: Princeton University Press.

Markheim, D. 2008. *America Should Support the Trans-Pacific Strategic Economic Partnership.* Web Memo 2178 (December). Washington, DC: Heritage Foundation.

Manchin, M., and A.O. Pelkmans-Balaoing. 2007. *Rules of Origin and the Web of East Asian Free Trade Agreements.* World Bank Policy Research Working Papers 4273 (July). Washington, DC: World Bank.

Mathews, J.A., and D.S. Cho. 2000. *Tiger Technology: The Creation of a Semi-Conductor Industry in East Asia.* Cambridge: Cambridge University Press.

Myrdal, G. 1968. *Asian Drama: An Inquiry into the Poverty of Nations,* 3 vols. New York: Twentieth Century Fund.

Petri, P. 2008. "Multitrack Integration in East Asian Trade: Noodle Bowl or Matrix?" *Asia Pacific Issues* 86 (October). Honolulu: East-West Center.

Petri, P., M. Plummer, and F. Zhai. 2011. *The Trans-Pacific Partnership and Asia-Pacific Integration: A Quantitative Assessment.* East-West Center Working Papers, Economic Series 119 (October). Honolulu: East-West Center.

Plummer, M. 2007. "Best Practices in Regional Trade Agreements: An Application to Asia." *World Economy* 30 (12): 1771–96.

Plummer, M., and G. Wignaraja. 2006. "The Post-Crisis Sequencing of Economic Integration in Asia: Trade as a Complement to a Monetary Future." *Economie Internationale* 107 (3): 59–85.

Sally, R. 2008. *New Frontiers in Free Trade: Globalization's Future and Asia's Rising Role.* Washington, DC: Cato Institute.

Stiglitz, J.E. 1996. "Some Lessons from the East Asian Miracle." *World Bank Research Observer* 11 (2): 151–77.

———. 2001. "From Miracle to Crisis to Recovery: Lessons from Four Decades of East Asian Experience." In *Rethinking the East Asian Miracle,* edited by J.E. Stiglitz and S. Yusuf. Oxford: Oxford University Press.

Takahashi, K., and S. Urata. 2008. *On the Use of FTAs by Japanese Firms.* RIETI Discussion Paper Series 08-E-002 (January). Tokyo: Research Institute for Economy, Trade and Industry.

Tran, B.C. 2012. "FTA Utilization and How to Support SMEs: Vietnam." Powerpoint presentation made at APEC Workshop on Increasing FTA Utilization by SMEs, Tokyo, Japan, August 7, 2012.

Tumbarello, P. 2007. *Are Regional Trade Agreements in Asia Stumbling Blocks or Building Blocks? Implications for Mekong-3 Countries.* IMF Working Paper WP/07/53 (March). Washington, DC: International Monetary Fund.

Udomwichaiwat, P. 2012. "Best Practices on FTA Promotion Policies: The Case of Thailand." Powerpoint presentation made at APEC Workshop on Increasing FTA Utilization by SMEs, Tokyo, Japan, August 7, 2012.

Urata, S. 2004. "The Emergence and Proliferation of Free Trade Agreements in East Asia." *Japanese Economy* 32 (2, Summer): 5–52.

Wade, R. 1990. *Governing the Market,* Princeton NJ: Princeton University Press.

Wignaraja. G. 2010. "Are ASEAN FTAs Used for Exporting?" In *Competitiveness of the ASEAN Countries: Corporate and Regulatory Drivers,* edited by P. Gugler and J. Chaisse. Cheltenham: Edward Elgar.

———. 2011. *Economic Reforms, Regionalism, and Exports: Comparing China and India.* Policy Studies 60. Honolulu: East West Center

———. 2012a. "Innovation, Learning and Exporting in China: Does R&D or a Technology Index Matter?" *Journal of Asian Economics* 23:224–33.

———. 2012b. "Commercial Policy and Experience in the Giants: China and India." In *The Oxford Handbook of International Commercial Policy,* edited by M. Kreinin and M. Plummer. Oxford: Oxford University Press.

Wignaraja. G., and D. Lazaro. 2010. *North-South vs. South–South Asian FTAs: Trends, Compatibilities, and Ways Forward.* UNU-CRIS Working Paper W-2010/3. Brugge, Belgium: UNU-CRIS.

Wignaraja. G., D. Ramizo, and L. Burmeister. 2012. *Asia–Latin America Free Trade Agreements: An Instrument for Inter-Regional Liberalization and Integration?* ADBI Working Paper Series 382 (September). Tokyo: Asian Development Bank Institute.

World Bank. 1993. *East Asian Miracle: Economic Growth and Public Policy.* Oxford: Oxford University Press.

———. 2007. *Trade Issues in East Asia: Preferential Rules of Origin.* Policy Research Report, East Asia and Pacific Region (Poverty Reduction and Economic Management). Washington, DC: World Bank.

WTO. 2011. *The WTO and Preferential Trade Agreements: From Co-existence to Coherence.* Geneva: World Trade Organization.

Zhang, Y. and M. Shen. 2011. *The Status of East Asian Free Trade Agreements.* ADBI Working Paper Series 282 (May). Tokyo: Asian Development Bank Institute.

Acknowledgments

The views expressed in this publication are the views of the authors and do not reflect the views or policies of ADB, the ADB Board of Directors, ADBI, or the governments they represent. We are most grateful to Edward Aspinall, Dieter Ernst, Mike Plummer, and two referees for comments; to Luca Burmeister, Dorothea Ramizo, and Anna-Mae Tuazon for research assistance; and to Elisa Johnston and Carol Wong for publications support.

www.ingramcontent.com/pod-product-compliance
Lightning Source LLC
Chambersburg PA
CBHW050551280326
41933CB00011B/1800